Build Your Career Guide

A Step-by-Step Plan for Beginners to Launch Their Dream Career

Harper Jameson

Table of Contents

Introduction

Why building a career is important for your future

As human beings, we all have dreams and aspirations. From a young age, we imagine ourselves doing great things, achieving our goals, and making a difference in the world. Our future is a blank canvas, waiting for us to fill it with our unique talents and passions. And building a career is one of the most important ways we can turn those dreams into reality.

A career is not just a job. It's a long-term journey that allows us to grow, develop new skills, and make a meaningful contribution to society. When we build a career, we're investing in ourselves and our future. We're committing to a path that will challenge us, inspire us, and ultimately help us become the best version of ourselves.

But why is building a career so important? Why can't we just work a series of jobs and call it a day? The answer lies in the many benefits that a career provides.

First and foremost, a career gives us a sense of purpose. When we have a career, we're working towards something greater than ourselves. We're using our skills and talents to make a difference in the world, whether that's through creating art, healing the sick, or designing buildings. When we have a sense of purpose, we're more motivated, engaged, and fulfilled in our work.

A career also provides us with financial stability. While money isn't everything, it's a necessary part of life. When we have a stable income, we can pay our bills, support our families, and save for the future. A career allows us to build wealth over time, which can give us more freedom and flexibility in our lives.

Moreover, a career helps us develop new skills and knowledge. When we're working in a particular field, we're constantly learning and growing. We're exposed to new ideas, technologies, and perspectives. We're challenged to think critically, solve problems, and collaborate with others. These skills can be applied not only in our work but in other areas of our lives as well.

A career also provides us with a sense of community. When we work with others who share our interests and passions, we form connections and relationships that can last a lifetime. We learn from our colleagues, share our experiences, and support each other through challenges. This sense of community can be incredibly rewarding and can help us feel like we're part of something larger than ourselves.

Finally, building a career allows us to leave a lasting legacy. When we look back on our lives, we want to know that we've made a difference. We want to leave the world a better place than we found it. A career provides us with an opportunity to do just that. Whether we're creating a new product, advocating for a cause, or helping others achieve their goals, we're leaving our mark on the world in a positive way.

Of course, building a career is not without its challenges. It requires hard work, perseverance, and a willingness to take risks. There will be setbacks, failures, and disappointments along the way. But with the right mindset and approach, these challenges can be overcome.

Building a career is one of the most important things we can do for ourselves and our future. It provides us with a sense of purpose, financial stability, new skills and knowledge, a sense of community, and the opportunity to leave a lasting legacy. So if you're considering building a career, don't hesitate. Take the first step today and start working towards your dreams. You never know where the journey may take you.

How this book can help you launch your dream career

If you're feeling lost, stuck, or unsure about your career path, you're not alone. Many people struggle with figuring out what they want to do for a living, or how to turn their dreams into reality. But the good news is that you don't have to go through this journey alone. That's where this book comes in.

"Build Your Career Guide: A Step-by-Step Plan for Beginners to Launch Their Dream Career" is a comprehensive guide that can help you build the foundation for a successful and fulfilling career. Whether you're just starting out in your career, or you're looking to make a change, this book provides a roadmap that can help you achieve your goals.

At its core, this book is about self-discovery. Before you can launch your dream career, you need to understand yourself - your skills, interests, values, and passions. Chapter One helps you do just that. Through a series of exercises and assessments, you'll gain clarity on what you bring to the table, what motivates you, and what you want out of your career.

But self-discovery is just the first step. Once you have a better understanding of yourself, it's time to explore your options. Chapter Two provides a roadmap for researching different industries and job roles, understanding the job market and trends, and identifying potential career paths that match your interests and skills.

Of course, finding your dream career is only half the battle. You also need to know how to navigate the job search process and stand out from the competition. That's where Chapters Three through Eight come in. These chapters cover everything from building a professional network and creating a winning resume, to writing effective cover letters, preparing for interviews, and negotiating job offers.

But landing a job is only the beginning. To succeed in your career, you need to continually develop your skills and find opportunities for growth and advancement. Chapters Nine and Ten provide guidance on developing in-demand skills, taking courses, attending workshops, and building strong relationships with colleagues and managers.

Of course, building a successful career is about more than just technical skills. It's also about managing your finances, maintaining work-life balance, and finding purpose and meaning in your work. Chapters Eleven through Fifteen cover these important topics, providing practical advice on budgeting, investing, prioritizing self-care and wellness, overcoming setbacks, staying up-to-date with industry trends, and making a positive impact on the world.

Throughout this book, you'll find actionable steps, real-world examples, and helpful tips to help you launch your dream career. But more than that, you'll find inspiration and encouragement to keep going, even when the journey gets tough. Because building a career is about more than just a paycheck - it's about finding your place in the world and making a meaningful contribution.

So if you're ready to take control of your career and start building the life you've always wanted, this book is for you. It's not a magic bullet, and it won't do the work for you. But it will provide the tools, guidance, and support you need to turn your dreams into reality.

Chapter One

Understanding Yourself

Assessing your skills, interests, and values

As you embark on your career journey, it's essential to take stock of your skills, interests, and values. These elements form the foundation of your career and determine the path you'll take. To achieve career success and fulfillment, it's vital to understand these aspects of yourself and use them to guide your decisions.

Assessing your skills is the first step towards building a career that aligns with your passions and abilities. Skills refer to the specific abilities you have acquired over time, whether through education, training, or experience. These skills can be technical, such as coding, writing, or project management, or soft skills, such as communication, problem-solving, and leadership.

One of the most effective ways to assess your skills is to conduct a skills inventory. A skills inventory involves listing all the skills you possess and rating them based on your level of proficiency. You can then identify areas where you need to improve or develop new skills to advance your career.

Your interests are another critical component of building a fulfilling career. Your interests are the activities, hobbies, or subjects that you enjoy and are passionate about. When you're engaged in activities that interest you, you're more likely to be motivated, productive, and satisfied. By contrast, working in a field that doesn't interest you can lead to boredom, burnout, and dissatisfaction.

To identify your interests, take some time to reflect on the activities that excite and energize you. Consider the topics you enjoy reading about or the hobbies you pursue in your spare time. Ask yourself what you would do if money were no object or what you would do if you had all the time in the world. Your answers to these questions can help you identify your true interests and guide your career decisions.

Values are the principles or beliefs that are most important to you. They guide your behavior and influence your decision-making. Your values can include things like honesty, integrity, compassion, or creativity. When your career aligns with your values, you're more likely to feel a sense of purpose and fulfillment.

To assess your values, reflect on the principles that are most important to you. Ask yourself what matters most in your life and what you stand for. Consider the values that guide your actions and how they align with your current career path. If your values and your career are not in alignment, it may be time to re-evaluate your goals and make changes.

Assessing your skills, interests, and values is not a one-time event. As you grow and evolve, your skills, interests, and values may change, requiring you to adjust your career path accordingly. Regularly checking in with yourself and reassessing these elements can help you stay on track and build a career that is both fulfilling and meaningful.

In conclusion, assessing your skills, interests, and values is the first step towards building a career that aligns with your passions and abilities. By understanding these aspects of yourself, you can make informed career decisions that lead to success and fulfillment. Whether you're just starting out or looking to make a career change, taking the time to reflect on your skills, interests, and values is an investment in your future. So, take a moment to assess where you are now and where you want to be. Your dream career is waiting for you.

Identifying your strengths and weaknesses

As you begin your dream career, it's important to take the time to think about your strengths and weaknesses. Knowing your strengths will allow you to focus on what you're good at and use those skills to succeed, while identifying your weaknesses will give you the ability to improve and overcome obstacles.

Identifying your strengths may seem like an easy task, but it requires a deep understanding of yourself and your abilities. You may be great at problem-solving, communication, or organization, or you may have a talent for creative thinking or leadership. Whatever your strengths may be, it's important to recognize them and use them to your advantage.

On the other hand, identifying your weaknesses can be a more challenging task. No one likes to admit they have weaknesses, but acknowledging them is the first step to improving and becoming a better version of yourself. It's important to remember that everyone has weaknesses, and it's not a sign of failure to acknowledge them.

One effective way to identify your strengths and weaknesses is to ask for feedback from others. This can be a humbling experience, but it can also be incredibly valuable. Ask your friends, family, colleagues, or mentors for honest feedback on your strengths and areas where you could improve. You may be surprised by what you learn and gain a new perspective on yourself.

Another way to identify your strengths and weaknesses is to reflect on your past experiences. Think about times when you felt successful and accomplished, and try to identify the skills and attributes that contributed to that success. Similarly, reflect on times when you struggled or faced challenges, and identify areas where you could have improved or where you felt lacking in skills or abilities.

Once you've identified your strengths and weaknesses, it's important to use that information to your advantage. If you know you excel at communication, for example, look for career opportunities that require strong communication skills. On the other hand, if you struggle with time management, focus on improving that skill and seek out resources or training to help you improve.

It's also important to remember that your strengths and weaknesses may change over time. As you gain new experiences and skills, your strengths may shift, and you may discover new weaknesses. It's important to regularly reassess your skills and abilities to ensure you're continuing to grow and develop in your career.

Identifying your strengths and weaknesses is not just about improving your career prospects, but it's also about developing a deeper understanding of yourself. By acknowledging your strengths and weaknesses, you'll gain a greater sense of self-awareness, which can help you make better decisions and live a more fulfilling life.

Identifying your strengths and weaknesses is an important step in building your dream career. It requires self-reflection, honesty, and a willingness to learn and improve. By recognizing your strengths, you can leverage them to achieve success, and by acknowledging your weaknesses, you can work on improving and overcoming obstacles. Remember that identifying your strengths and weaknesses is an ongoing process, and it's important to regularly reassess your skills and abilities to continue growing and developing in your career.

Setting career goals that align with your passions and purpose

As human beings, we all have a purpose in life. We have unique talents, interests, and passions that make us who we are. When we are able to identify and align these elements with our career goals, we are more likely to achieve success and fulfillment in our professional lives.

Setting career goals that align with our passions and purpose is a crucial step in building a career that we love. However, it can be a daunting task, especially for those just starting out in their careers. Many people struggle with figuring out what they really want to do or what their true purpose is.

One way to begin identifying career goals that align with our passions and purpose is to reflect on our past experiences. What have been some of our most rewarding experiences, both in and out of the workplace? What are some of the things we are naturally good at and enjoy doing? These are important clues that can help us identify our strengths and interests.

Another important step is to explore various career options and industries. It's important to do research and gain a deep understanding of the different jobs and industries available. This includes learning about the qualifications and skills required for different positions, the job outlook and growth potential, and the work culture and values of different companies.

While exploring different career options, it's also important to ask ourselves what kind of impact we want to make in our careers. Do we want to make a difference in the lives of others? Do we want to work towards a specific cause or mission? By answering these questions, we can begin to narrow down our career goals and identify paths that align with our passions and purpose.

Once we have identified our career goals, it's important to set specific, measurable, and realistic targets. This could include setting deadlines for achieving certain milestones or breaking down long-term goals into smaller, achievable steps. By setting clear goals, we can stay focused and motivated as we work towards building the career of our dreams.

However, it's important to keep in mind that career goals are not set in stone. As we grow and evolve as individuals, our goals may also change. It's important to remain flexible and open to new opportunities that align with our passions and purpose.

In addition to setting career goals, it's also important to have a plan in place for achieving those goals. This includes identifying the resources and support we need to succeed. This may include seeking out mentors or networking with industry professionals who can offer guidance and advice, or enrolling in courses or workshops to develop new skills.

It's also important to recognize that building a career is a journey, and there will be setbacks and challenges along the way. It's important to stay resilient and focused, and to seek out support and resources when needed. This may include seeking out a therapist or counselor to help manage stress and anxiety, or seeking out peer support groups or networking events to connect with others in our field.

In conclusion, setting career goals that align with our passions and purpose is a crucial step in building a career that we love. By reflecting on our past experiences, exploring different career options, and setting specific and achievable targets, we can work towards achieving our dreams. While the journey may not always be easy, by remaining focused, flexible, and resilient, we can build a career that not only brings us professional success, but also personal fulfillment and purpose.

Chapter Two

Exploring Career Options

Researching different industries and job roles

Researching different industries and job roles is a crucial step in the process of building a successful career. It is important to have a clear understanding of the job market, including the current trends and demands, in order to make informed decisions about your career path.

The first step in researching different industries and job roles is to identify your skills, interests, and values. This information can help you narrow down your options and focus on industries that align with your personal and professional goals. Once you have a general idea of the industries that interest you, it's time to dig deeper and explore specific job roles within those industries.

One way to research different industries and job roles is to utilize online resources, such as job boards and industry-specific websites. These resources can provide valuable information about current job openings, required qualifications, and salary ranges. You can also use social media platforms to connect with professionals in your desired field and gain insights into their experiences.

Another way to research different industries and job roles is to attend industry events and conferences. These events provide a great opportunity to network with professionals in your desired field, learn about current industry trends, and gain insights into specific job roles. You may also consider reaching out to alumni from your college or university who work in the industries or job roles you are interested in. They can provide valuable advice and guidance based on their own experiences.

It is important to keep an open mind during the research process and consider industries and job roles that may not be immediately obvious. For example, you may have skills and interests that could be applied to a variety of industries, so it's important to consider all your options before making a decision.

In addition to researching different industries and job roles, it's important to consider the job market and demand for specific positions. Some industries may have high demand for certain roles, while others may have limited opportunities. By understanding the job market, you can make informed decisions about your career path and ensure that you are pursuing a field with ample opportunities for growth and advancement.

It's also important to consider the future of the industry and how it may evolve over time. Some industries may be experiencing rapid growth and change, while others may be declining or becoming obsolete. By staying up-to-date with industry trends and projections, you can ensure that you are making informed decisions about your career path and positioning yourself for long-term success.

Ultimately, researching different industries and job roles is an important step in building a successful career. By gaining insights into different industries and job roles, you can identify opportunities that align with your skills, interests, and values, and position yourself for success in the job market. Remember to keep an open mind, stay informed about industry trends, and seek out advice and guidance from professionals in your desired field. With the right approach, you can build a fulfilling and successful career that aligns with your passions and purpose.

Understanding the job market and trends

The job market can be a complex and constantly evolving entity, influenced by a variety of factors ranging from economic conditions to emerging technologies. As a job seeker, it's important to understand the job market and trends in order to make informed decisions about your career path and job search strategies.

One of the key factors that can influence the job market is the state of the economy. During times of economic growth, job opportunities may increase across a wide range of industries, while during times of economic downturn, job opportunities may be more limited. In addition, certain industries may be more affected than others during economic fluctuations, such as the hospitality and tourism industries during a pandemic.

Another important factor in understanding the job market is knowing which industries and job roles are in demand.

Emerging technologies and changing consumer preferences can lead to shifts in the job market, creating new opportunities in some areas while reducing demand in others. For example, the rise of e-commerce has led to an increase in demand for jobs in logistics and delivery, while reducing demand for jobs in traditional brick-and-mortar retail.

Researching job market trends can help you identify which industries and job roles are likely to experience growth in the coming years, allowing you to make informed decisions about your career path. Some resources for researching job market trends include industry publications, government reports, and labor market data.

In addition to understanding the overall job market, it's also important to research individual companies and job roles to gain a better understanding of the specific requirements and expectations of each position. This can involve researching job descriptions and company profiles, as well as networking with individuals who currently work in your target industry or job role.

One key trend in the job market is the growing importance of soft skills, such as communication, collaboration, and problem-solving. While technical skills are still important in many industries, employers are increasingly looking for candidates who have a strong combination of technical and soft skills. This means that job seekers should not only focus on developing technical skills related to their chosen field, but also on developing strong communication, teamwork, and problem-solving abilities.

Another trend in the job market is the growing demand for remote work and flexible schedules. The COVID-19 pandemic has accelerated this trend, with many companies shifting to remote work models in order to protect employee health and safety. As a result, job seekers may find more opportunities for remote work or flexible schedules in the current job market.

Finally, it's important to keep in mind that the job market is constantly evolving, and trends may change rapidly over time. As a job seeker, it's important to stay up-to-date on the latest job market trends and adjust your job search strategies accordingly.

Understanding the job market and trends is a critical component of building a successful career. By researching job market trends and staying up-to-date on the latest developments in your chosen industry or job role, you can make informed decisions about your career path and job search strategies. Remember, the job market is constantly evolving, so it's important to remain flexible and adaptable as you pursue your dream career.

Identifying potential career paths that match your interests and skills

As you move forward in your career journey, it is essential to explore various career paths that align with your interests and skills. By doing so, you will be able to identify career options that can provide you with a fulfilling and meaningful professional life.

Identifying potential career paths that match your interests and skills can be a daunting task, but it is crucial to take the time to explore various options. You may have a clear idea of what you want to do, but it's always worth considering other possibilities that you may not have thought of before.

One of the first steps in identifying potential career paths is to assess your skills and interests. You can begin by asking yourself some fundamental questions, such as:

- What are my passions and interests?
- What skills do I have that I enjoy using?
- What type of work do I find most rewarding?
- What are my natural talents and strengths?
- What motivates me to succeed?

Answering these questions can help you gain insight into the type of work you enjoy and the skills you excel at. This can help you identify potential career paths that align with your interests and strengths.

Next, you can research various industries and job roles to see which ones may be a good fit for you. You can do this by reading job descriptions, researching industry trends, and talking to people who work in various fields.

One helpful resource for identifying potential career paths is the Occupational Outlook Handbook, which provides in-depth information on job growth, salaries, and necessary education and training for different occupations.

Once you have identified potential career paths, it is important to evaluate whether they align with your values and long-term goals. You may find that some careers are a better match for your lifestyle or offer more opportunities for growth and development.

It's also essential to consider the job market for your chosen career path. You may have a passion for a specific industry, but if the job market is saturated or declining, it may be challenging to find stable employment. In contrast, industries with growing demand and job opportunities may provide more long-term career stability.

In addition to researching job roles and industries, networking can also be a valuable tool for identifying potential career paths. Connecting with professionals in your desired field can provide you with insider information on job requirements, industry trends, and potential career paths. Attending industry events, joining professional organizations, and following industry leaders on social media can help you build a robust professional network.

Finally, don't be afraid to take calculated risks and try new things. Your career journey may not always be a straight line, and it's okay to pivot and change direction as you gain new experiences and insights. Sometimes the most unexpected opportunities can lead to the most rewarding careers.

Identifying potential career paths that match your interests and skills is a critical step in launching your dream career. By assessing your skills and interests, researching various industries and job roles, and networking with professionals in your desired field, you can gain valuable insights into potential career paths. Remember to consider your values and long-term goals, and don't be afraid to take calculated risks and try new things. With time, patience, and determination, you can identify a career path that provides you with fulfillment and purpose.

Chapter Three

Building a Professional Network

Developing a personal brand

In today's job market, standing out from the crowd is more important than ever. With the rise of social media and online networking, it's crucial to have a personal brand that accurately reflects who you are and what you have to offer. Developing a personal brand can help you differentiate yourself from other job candidates, showcase your unique skills and experiences, and ultimately help you land your dream job.

So, what exactly is a personal brand? Simply put, it's the way you present yourself to the world. It encompasses everything from your online presence to your communication style to the way you dress. Your personal brand is what people think of when they hear your name or see your face.

Developing a personal brand starts with understanding who you are and what you stand for. Start by identifying your core values, your unique strengths and talents, and your career goals. Then, think about how you want to be perceived by others. Do you want to be seen as a thought leader in your industry? Do you want to be known for your creativity and innovation? Whatever your goals, your personal brand should be a reflection of your authentic self.

Once you have a clear understanding of who you are and what you stand for, it's time to start building your brand. One of the most important elements of your personal brand is your online presence. This includes your website, social media profiles, and any other online platforms you use. Make sure your profiles are consistent across all platforms, with a clear and professional headshot and a concise summary of who you are and what you do.

When it comes to social media, be intentional about what you post and share. Share articles and resources that are relevant to your industry or area of expertise, and engage with other thought leaders in your field. Use hashtags to help people find your content and participate in online conversations related to your industry.

Beyond your online presence, your personal brand should also be reflected in the way you communicate and present yourself in person. Dress professionally and appropriately for the situation, and pay attention to your body language and tone of voice. Develop your communication skills so that you can clearly and confidently articulate your ideas and expertise.

Another key element of your personal brand is your network. Building strong relationships with others in your industry can help you gain visibility and credibility, as well as open up new opportunities. Attend industry events and conferences, join professional organizations, and network online through platforms like LinkedIn. Be generous with your time and expertise, and offer to help others whenever you can.

Finally, remember that building a personal brand is an ongoing process. As you gain new skills and experiences, your brand may evolve and change over time. Continuously evaluate your online presence, communication style, and professional network to ensure that they align with your goals and values.

In summary, developing a personal brand is a critical component of building a successful career in today's job market. By understanding who you are, building a strong online presence, honing your communication skills, and cultivating a strong professional network, you can create a personal brand that accurately reflects your unique skills and experiences, and sets you apart from the competition.

Building relationships with mentors, peers, and industry experts

Success is never achieved alone. Building meaningful relationships with mentors, peers, and industry experts is a vital step towards launching a successful career. These relationships can provide valuable insights, guidance, and support as you navigate the complexities of your chosen field. In this article, we will explore the importance of building relationships with these key individuals and how they can help you achieve your career goals.

Mentors are experienced professionals who can guide you through the ups and downs of your career journey. They can offer advice, share their experiences, and help you make informed decisions. Mentors can come from a variety of backgrounds and can be found through networking events, industry associations, or even social media. When selecting a mentor, it is important to find someone who has experience in your chosen field and who shares your values and goals.

Peers are another essential source of support in your career journey. Your peers are those individuals who are at a similar stage in their careers and who share similar interests and goals. They can provide you with valuable feedback, offer new perspectives, and help you stay motivated. Additionally, building relationships with your peers can lead to new job opportunities, collaborations, and partnerships in the future.

Industry experts are individuals who have established themselves as leaders in your chosen field. They are often sought-after speakers and contributors to industry publications. Building a relationship with an industry expert can provide you with access to valuable insights, networking opportunities, and career advice. These individuals can also serve as a source of inspiration and motivation, helping you to stay on track and achieve your goals.

So how do you build these relationships? The key is to be proactive and to invest time and effort in cultivating meaningful connections. Here are some tips to help you get started:

1. Attend industry events: Industry events are a great way to meet new people and learn about the latest trends and developments in your field. Look for conferences, seminars, and networking events that align with your interests and make a point to attend them regularly.

2. Join industry associations: Joining an industry association is an excellent way to connect with like-minded professionals and stay up-to-date with industry news and developments. Many associations also offer mentorship programs, which can be a great way to connect with experienced professionals in your field.

3. Use social media: Social media platforms like LinkedIn, Twitter, and Instagram can be powerful tools for building your professional network. Connect with people in your field, share your work and ideas, and engage with others in meaningful ways.

4. Offer value: Building relationships is a two-way street. Look for ways to offer value to the people in your network by sharing your knowledge, expertise, and resources. This can help you establish yourself as a valuable member of your community and can lead to new opportunities down the road.

5. Be genuine: Authenticity is key when building relationships. Be yourself, show interest in others, and make a genuine effort to get to know the people in your network. This can help you build trust and establish lasting connections.

Building relationships with mentors, peers, and industry experts is an essential step towards launching a successful career. These relationships can provide you with valuable insights, guidance, and support as you navigate your chosen field. By being proactive, investing time and effort, and offering value to others, you can build meaningful connections that will help you achieve your goals and fulfill your potential.

Leveraging social media and online platforms to expand your network

In today's digital age, social media has become a vital tool for networking and building professional relationships. Platforms such as LinkedIn, Twitter, and Instagram offer individuals the opportunity to connect with others in their industry, gain visibility, and showcase their expertise. If you're looking to expand your network, social media is a great place to start.

LinkedIn is often considered the most important platform for professional networking. It's a platform where you can connect with colleagues, industry experts, and potential employers. You can use it to build your personal brand, showcase your skills and experience, and find new job opportunities. To leverage LinkedIn effectively, make sure your profile is up-to-date and complete. Use a professional headshot and a clear headline that highlights your skills and experience. Also, make sure to include a summary that explains who you are and what you do.

Another great platform for networking is Twitter. It's a great place to engage with other professionals in your industry, share your thoughts and ideas, and stay up-to-date on industry news and trends. To get the most out of Twitter, start by following influencers and thought leaders in your field. Engage with their content by retweeting, commenting, and sharing their posts. This will help you get noticed and start building relationships with people in your industry.

Instagram is a platform that's often overlooked when it comes to professional networking. However, it can be a great place to showcase your creativity and build your personal brand. If you're in a creative field, such as design or photography, Instagram is a great place to showcase your work and connect with others in your industry. You can use hashtags to make your content more discoverable and engage with others by commenting and liking their posts.

In addition to social media, there are several online platforms that can help you expand your network. One of these is Meetup.com, which is a platform that connects people with similar interests. You can use it to find local events and meetups that are relevant to your industry or career goals. Attending these events is a great way to meet new people, learn new skills, and expand your network.

Another platform worth considering is Quora. Quora is a question-and-answer platform where people can ask and answer questions on a wide range of topics. By answering questions related to your industry, you can showcase your expertise and build your personal brand. You can also use Quora to connect with other professionals in your field and engage in discussions related to your industry.

When it comes to networking online, it's important to remember that it's not just about building a large network. It's also about building meaningful relationships with people in your industry. Take the time to engage with others, share your expertise, and offer value whenever possible. This will help you build a reputation as a trusted and knowledgeable professional, which can open up new opportunities down the road.

Leveraging social media and online platforms is a great way to expand your network and build relationships with others in your industry. Whether you're using LinkedIn to connect with colleagues and potential employers, Twitter to engage with influencers and thought leaders, or Instagram to showcase your creativity, there are plenty of opportunities to connect with others online. By taking the time to engage with others, share your expertise, and offer value, you can build meaningful relationships that can help you achieve your career goals.

Chapter Four

Creating a Winning Resume

Crafting a compelling resume that highlights your achievements and skills

In today's competitive job market, having a strong and compelling resume is essential to stand out from the crowd. A well-crafted resume is your ticket to securing an interview and ultimately landing your dream job. But how do you create a resume that truly showcases your achievements and skills?

The first step in crafting a compelling resume is to understand its purpose. A resume is not just a list of your past experiences and education; it is a marketing tool designed to demonstrate why you are the best fit for the job you are applying for. To achieve this goal, your resume must effectively communicate your unique value proposition to potential employers.

One key element of a successful resume is a clear and concise professional summary. This brief section should highlight your most impressive achievements and skills, and provide a snapshot of your experience and expertise. Avoid generic or cliché statements and instead focus on specific accomplishments that demonstrate your capabilities.

When it comes to listing your work experience, be sure to focus on your achievements rather than just your responsibilities. Use action verbs and quantitative data to highlight your impact on previous projects and organizations. For example, instead of simply stating that you managed a team, quantify the number of team members and describe how you successfully led them to achieve specific goals.

Another important aspect of a strong resume is showcasing your relevant skills and certifications. Be sure to highlight any certifications or professional development courses you have completed, and emphasize your technical and soft skills that align with the job requirements.

In addition to highlighting your accomplishments and skills, your resume should also be visually appealing and easy to read. Use a clean and professional font, and make sure the formatting is consistent throughout the document. Use bullet points and white space to break up large blocks of text and make the content more digestible.

One common mistake job seekers make on their resumes is including irrelevant information. Keep in mind that employers are typically looking for candidates who have experience and skills directly related to the job requirements. Therefore, it's important to tailor your resume to each specific job you apply for. This means carefully reviewing the job posting and customizing your resume to highlight the skills and experiences that are most relevant to the position.

Finally, proofread your resume carefully to ensure that there are no errors or typos. Even a small mistake can be a red flag for potential employers, so take the time to review your resume thoroughly.

Crafting a compelling resume that highlights your achievements and skills requires a combination of strategic thinking, strong writing skills, and attention to detail. By focusing on your unique value proposition, highlighting your relevant experiences and skills, and customizing your resume to each job you apply for, you can create a document that effectively showcases your professional abilities and helps you stand out in the competitive job market.

Customizing your resume for different job applications

A resume is an essential document that represents your professional self to potential employers. It highlights your skills, achievements, and experience and serves as the first impression for hiring managers. A well-crafted resume can make all the difference in landing your dream job, but not all resumes are created equal. Customizing your resume for different job applications is an important step in ensuring that your application stands out from the crowd.

Customizing your resume means tailoring it to fit the specific requirements of the job you are applying for. It involves analyzing the job description and identifying the key skills and qualifications that the employer is looking for. By doing this, you can showcase your relevant experience and skills and demonstrate why you are the best fit for the position.

To start customizing your resume, you should begin by thoroughly reviewing the job posting. Look for keywords and phrases that describe the responsibilities, qualifications, and desired traits for the position. Take note of the required experience, education, and certifications, as well as any soft skills, such as communication or leadership abilities. These will be the building blocks of your customized resume.

Next, consider how your experience and skills align with the job requirements. Identify your relevant experience, accomplishments, and qualifications that directly relate to the position. Use concrete examples and metrics to demonstrate your proficiency and showcase your achievements.

Once you have identified your relevant experience and skills, you can start to tailor your resume. Begin by customizing your summary or objective statement to reflect the job you are applying for. This should be a brief statement that highlights your relevant experience and skills and how they align with the position.

Next, modify the bullet points in your work experience section to emphasize the skills and accomplishments that align with the job requirements. Use active verbs to describe your accomplishments and quantify your results wherever possible. For example, instead of simply stating that you "managed a team," use specific metrics to describe how you led and motivated your team to achieve specific goals.

In addition to customizing your work experience section, you should also tailor your skills and education sections. Make sure to include any relevant certifications or coursework that demonstrate your proficiency in the skills required for the job.

Finally, be sure to proofread your customized resume carefully before submitting it. Review it multiple times to ensure that there are no errors or typos, and that it accurately reflects your skills and experience.

Customizing your resume for different job applications can be a time-consuming process, but it is well worth the effort. By tailoring your resume to fit the specific requirements of the job, you can demonstrate your qualifications and stand out from other applicants. It shows that you have taken the time to understand the job and that you are committed to securing the position.

Customizing your resume is an essential step in the job application process. It allows you to showcase your relevant experience and skills and demonstrate why you are the best fit for the position. By analyzing the job posting, identifying your relevant experience and skills, and tailoring your resume accordingly, you can increase your chances of landing your dream job.

Leveraging resume templates and tools to streamline the process

As you begin your job search, one of the most important tools you'll need is a well-crafted resume. While the process of creating a resume can be daunting, there are tools and templates available that can streamline the process and help you create a professional-looking document that highlights your skills and achievements.

Resume templates are pre-designed layouts that you can customize to suit your needs. They often come with pre-written sections that you can fill in with your own information, such as your name, contact information, education, work experience, and skills. Templates can save you time and effort, as they eliminate the need to start from scratch and design your own layout.

There are a wide variety of resume templates available online, ranging from simple and clean designs to more creative and unique layouts. When selecting a template, consider the industry you are applying to and choose a design that fits the job requirements and company culture.

One important thing to keep in mind when using a template is to customize it to fit your own unique experience and skills. While a template can provide a strong foundation for your resume, it is important to tailor it to highlight your specific qualifications for the job you are applying for.

Another tool that can be helpful in the resume-building process is a resume builder. Resume builders are online tools that guide you through the process of creating a resume, often using a template as a starting point. They provide prompts and suggestions for each section of the resume, helping you to craft a document that showcases your skills and experiences in a clear and concise way.

Resume builders are especially helpful for those who are new to the job market or who may be struggling to organize their work experience and achievements. They can also be useful for those who are looking to create multiple resumes for different job applications, as many builders allow you to save and customize multiple versions of your resume.

When using a resume builder, it is still important to customize your resume to fit the job requirements and highlight your unique qualifications. Be sure to review and edit the information provided by the builder to ensure that it accurately represents your skills and experiences.

In addition to templates and builders, there are also online tools available that can help you optimize your resume for applicant tracking systems (ATS). ATS is software used by many companies to screen and filter resumes based on certain keywords and qualifications. By using an ATS-friendly template or tool, you can increase your chances of getting past the initial screening and into the hands of a human recruiter.

It is important to remember that while resume templates and tools can be helpful, they should not be relied on entirely. It is crucial to review and edit your resume to ensure that it accurately reflects your skills and experiences, and to tailor it to each specific job application.

Using a resume template or builder can be an effective way to streamline the process of creating a professional-looking resume. However, it is important to remember to customize your resume to fit the job requirements and to showcase your unique skills and experiences. By leveraging these tools and taking the time to create a tailored resume, you can increase your chances of standing out to potential employers and landing the job of your dreams.

Chapter Five

Writing Effective Cover Letters

Understanding the purpose of cover letters and how to make them stand out

When it comes to job applications, many job seekers focus heavily on crafting the perfect resume. While a strong resume is important, it's equally important to give the same level of attention to your cover letter. A cover letter is your chance to make a great first impression and demonstrate your enthusiasm and qualifications for the position. In this article, we'll discuss the purpose of cover letters and how to make them stand out from the crowd.

First and foremost, it's important to understand the purpose of a cover letter. Your cover letter should serve as an introduction to your resume, highlighting your skills, experiences, and qualifications that make you the best fit for the job. It's also an opportunity to showcase your personality and demonstrate your enthusiasm for the position and the company.

When crafting your cover letter, the first step is to carefully read the job description and company information. This will help you tailor your cover letter to the specific job and company, making it more likely to stand out to the hiring manager. You should also research the company culture and values to ensure that your cover letter reflects their mission and values.

Next, start your cover letter with a strong opening that grabs the hiring manager's attention. You can do this by mentioning a recent accomplishment of the company, or by sharing a personal story that demonstrates your passion for the job. Make sure to address the hiring manager by name, if possible, and introduce yourself and your qualifications for the job.

The body of your cover letter should highlight your most relevant experiences and accomplishments. Use specific examples to demonstrate how your skills and experiences align with the job requirements. Avoid repeating information from your resume; instead, use the cover letter to expand upon the most important qualifications and experiences.

In addition to highlighting your qualifications, it's important to convey your enthusiasm for the position and the company. Show the hiring manager that you've done your research and are excited about the opportunity to contribute to the company's success. You can also mention any personal connections you have to the company or industry, such as a shared passion for a particular cause or interest.

When wrapping up your cover letter, make sure to express your gratitude for the opportunity to apply for the position. Restate your interest in the job and your enthusiasm for the company, and invite the hiring manager to contact you to schedule an interview. Finally, close with a professional sign-off, such as "Sincerely" or "Best regards."

To make your cover letter stand out from the crowd, it's important to avoid common mistakes that can hurt your chances of getting hired. First and foremost, make sure to proofread your cover letter carefully for spelling and grammar errors. A sloppy or error-filled cover letter can make a poor impression on the hiring manager.

Another common mistake is to use a generic or one-size-fits-all cover letter. Instead, take the time to tailor your cover letter to the specific job and company. Use specific examples and language that aligns with the job requirements and company culture.

Finally, make sure to follow the application instructions carefully. Some job postings may require specific formatting or documents, such as a writing sample or references. Failure to follow these instructions can demonstrate a lack of attention to detail and hurt your chances of getting hired.

A strong cover letter is an essential part of any job application. By understanding the purpose of a cover letter and taking the time to tailor it to the specific job and company, you can make a great first impression and stand out from the crowd. Remember to highlight your most relevant experiences and accomplishments, convey your enthusiasm for the position, and avoid common mistakes that can hurt your chances of getting hired. With these tips, you'll be well on your way to crafting a winning cover letter that gets you noticed by hiring managers.

Tailoring your cover letter to the job description and company culture

Your cover letter is your first opportunity to make a great impression on a potential employer. It's your chance to demonstrate your interest in the job and the company and to showcase your skills and experience. But to truly stand out, your cover letter needs to be tailored to the job description and the company culture.

Tailoring your cover letter means customizing it to the specific job you're applying for. This requires careful attention to the job description and the requirements listed. Your cover letter should highlight how your skills and experience match the requirements listed in the job posting. Use specific examples to illustrate your qualifications and show how you can add value to the company.

But tailoring your cover letter goes beyond just matching your skills to the job requirements. You also need to consider the company culture and values. This means researching the company and understanding its mission, vision, and goals. Look for clues in the job posting or on the company's website about the company culture, such as its values, work environment, and employee benefits.

Once you've researched the company, incorporate this knowledge into your cover letter. Use language that aligns with the company's values and mission. For example, if the company prides itself on innovation, use language that demonstrates your own innovative thinking and problem-solving skills. If the company has a strong focus on teamwork, highlight your experience working collaboratively with others.

Another way to tailor your cover letter to the company culture is to use industry-specific language. This shows that you're knowledgeable about the industry and that you understand the company's role within it. Use industry-specific terms and jargon, but be careful not to overdo it. You want to demonstrate your expertise without sounding like you're trying too hard.

In addition to language, you can also tailor the format and style of your cover letter to the company culture. For example, if the company is known for its creativity and innovation, you might consider using a non-traditional format or incorporating some design elements into your cover letter. If the company is more traditional, you might want to stick with a more formal format and tone.

But tailoring your cover letter isn't just about impressing the employer – it's also about showing that you're a good fit for the company. By demonstrating that you've done your research and that you understand the company culture and values, you're showing that you're serious about the job and that you're invested in the company's success.

To ensure that your cover letter is tailored to the job description and company culture, here are some steps you can follow:

1. Research the company: Visit the company's website and social media pages, read news articles about the company, and look for reviews from current or former employees.

2. Analyze the job posting: Read the job posting carefully and highlight the requirements and qualifications listed. Look for keywords that you can use in your cover letter.

3. Customize your content: Use the information you've gathered to customize your cover letter. Use specific examples to demonstrate how your skills and experience match the requirements listed in the job posting.

4. Use language that aligns with the company culture: Incorporate language that aligns with the company's values, mission, and goals. Use industry-specific language to show that you're knowledgeable about the industry.

5. Tailor the format and style: Consider the company culture and values when choosing the format and style of your cover letter. Use a non-traditional format or design elements if the company is known for its creativity and innovation.

Tailoring your cover letter to the job description and company culture is essential if you want to stand out from other applicants.

Avoiding common mistakes that can hurt your chances of getting hired

When it comes to the job search process, there are few things more daunting than putting together a strong job application. From crafting a winning resume to writing a compelling cover letter, every piece of the puzzle plays a role in convincing potential employers that you're the right fit for the job. However, even the most impressive qualifications and accomplishments can be overshadowed by common mistakes that can hurt your chances of getting hired.

One of the most common mistakes job seekers make is submitting a generic or one-size-fits-all cover letter. A cover letter should be tailored to the specific job and company you're applying to, showcasing how your skills and experience make you the ideal candidate for that particular role. Failing to do so can signal to employers that you're not particularly interested in the position or the company, and that you're just looking for any job that comes your way.

Another mistake to avoid is simply regurgitating your resume in your cover letter. Your cover letter should complement your resume, not repeat it. Rather than simply listing your qualifications and work experience, use your cover letter to tell a story about your professional journey and highlight the most relevant accomplishments that make you a strong fit for the job.

It's also important to avoid using vague or clichéd language in your cover letter. Phrases like "hardworking," "detail-oriented," and "team player" may sound good in theory, but they don't actually tell the employer much about your qualifications or experience. Instead, use specific examples to demonstrate how you embody these qualities and how they have helped you succeed in past roles.

Another common mistake is failing to proofread your cover letter for spelling and grammar errors. A single typo can make a poor impression on employers and suggest that you don't pay attention to details. Take the time to carefully review your cover letter before submitting it, and consider having a friend or mentor look it over as well.

Another mistake that can hurt your chances of getting hired is failing to address the hiring manager by name in your cover letter. A generic greeting like "To whom it may concern" or "Dear hiring manager" can come across as impersonal and suggest that you didn't do your research on the company or position. Take the time to research the company and find out who the hiring manager or recruiter is, and address them directly in your cover letter.

Finally, avoid making unrealistic or grandiose claims in your cover letter. While it's important to showcase your strengths and accomplishments, making exaggerated statements can come across as insincere or untrustworthy. Stick to the facts and provide specific examples of your qualifications and experience, and let your achievements speak for themselves.

In summary, there are many common mistakes that job seekers make in their cover letters that can hurt their chances of getting hired. To avoid these mistakes, tailor your cover letter to the specific job and company, avoid using generic or clichéd language, proofread carefully, address the hiring manager by name, and be honest and straightforward about your qualifications and experience. By taking the time to craft a thoughtful and compelling cover letter, you can increase your chances of standing out from the competition and landing your dream job.

Chapter Six

Preparing for Interviews

Understanding different types of job interviews and how to prepare for them

Job interviews can be a nerve-wracking experience, but being well-prepared can help alleviate some of the stress. One important aspect of preparation is understanding the different types of job interviews and how to prepare for them. Here, we'll explore some common types of job interviews and share tips on how to best prepare for each one.

1. Phone Interviews
    Phone interviews are often used as an initial screening tool before inviting candidates for an in-person interview. They are typically brief and can range from 10 to 30 minutes. During a phone interview, the interviewer is usually trying to get a sense of your communication skills, basic qualifications, and interest in the position.

To prepare for a phone interview, make sure you are in a quiet and distraction-free environment. Have your resume, job description, and any notes you've taken on the company or role in front of you. Speak clearly and confidently, and try to convey your enthusiasm for the position.

2. Video Interviews

Video interviews have become more common in recent years, especially with the rise of remote work. They can be conducted through a variety of platforms, such as Zoom, Skype, or Google Meet. Like phone interviews, video interviews are often used as an initial screening tool, but they allow the interviewer to get a better sense of your non-verbal communication and personality.

To prepare for a video interview, test your equipment and internet connection beforehand. Choose a well-lit and quiet location, and make sure your background is clean and professional. Dress appropriately and make eye contact with the interviewer. Also, try to avoid looking at yourself on the screen, as this can be distracting.

3. Behavioral Interviews

    Behavioral interviews are designed to assess how you have handled specific situations in the past, and are often used to evaluate your problem-solving skills and decision-making abilities. During a behavioral interview, the interviewer will ask you to provide examples of situations you've faced and how you handled them.

To prepare for a behavioral interview, review the job description and company values to get an idea of what kinds of situations they may be interested in. Think about specific examples from your past experiences that demonstrate your skills and accomplishments. Use the STAR method (Situation, Task, Action, Result) to structure your answers and provide context.

4. Panel Interviews

    Panel interviews involve multiple interviewers, and are often used in situations where the role would require interaction with multiple people or departments. Panel interviews can be more challenging, as you need to engage with multiple people at once and address different perspectives and questions.

To prepare for a panel interview, research the interviewers and their roles in advance. Take notes during the interview to keep track of who asked what questions, and address each person by name when answering. Try to stay calm and focused, and make sure to maintain eye contact with each panelist.

5. Case Interviews
   Case interviews are common in fields such as consulting and finance, and involve solving a hypothetical problem or scenario. Case interviews are designed to evaluate your analytical and problem-solving skills, as well as your ability to communicate your thought process.

To prepare for a case interview, practice solving sample cases and working through them out loud. Use frameworks to organize your thinking and stay structured. Don't be afraid to ask clarifying questions, and make sure to communicate your assumptions and reasoning clearly.

In conclusion, understanding the different types of job interviews and how to prepare for them can help you feel more confident and prepared during the interview process. Research the company and role, practice answering common interview questions, and be prepared to demonstrate your skills and accomplishments. With a little preparation, you can ace your next job interview and land the job of your dreams.

Researching the company and the interviewer

Researching the company and the interviewer is a crucial step in preparing for any job interview. It demonstrates your interest in the company and your dedication to the position you are applying for. By doing your research, you can also gain valuable insights into the company's culture, values, and goals, which can help you tailor your answers and make a stronger impression during the interview.

First, start with the company's website. Look for information on their mission, vision, and values. Read about their products or services, and try to understand their position in the market. Check out their social media profiles, including LinkedIn, Twitter, and Facebook, to see what they are sharing with their followers. This can give you a better sense of their brand and how they engage with their audience.

Another helpful resource is news articles and industry reports. Look for recent news about the company, such as acquisitions, new product launches, or partnerships. This information can give you an idea of the company's priorities and where they are headed. Additionally, researching the industry can provide context for the company's position within the market and help you better understand their challenges and opportunities.

Next, research the interviewer if possible. Check LinkedIn or other professional networking sites to see if you can find their profile. Look for commonalities between your background and experience and their own. This can help you connect with them on a personal level during the interview. You may also gain insight into their role at the company and what they may be looking for in a candidate.

During your research, pay attention to any potential red flags. Look for information about the company's reputation, any legal or ethical issues they have faced, or negative reviews from employees or customers. This information can be a warning sign that the company may not be the best fit for you.

Once you have gathered your research, use it to prepare for the interview. Incorporate the company's mission and values into your answers, and use specific examples of how your skills and experience align with their goals. Reference recent news or developments in the company to demonstrate your interest and knowledge of the industry.

If you have identified the interviewer, use your research to personalize your responses. For example, if you see that they have worked on a particular project, mention it in your answer and ask for their thoughts. This can demonstrate your interest in their work and build a rapport with the interviewer.

In addition to researching the company and the interviewer, make sure to also prepare for common interview questions. Practice your responses and consider your body language and tone of voice. Dress professionally and arrive early to ensure you have time to compose yourself before the interview.

By taking the time to research the company and the interviewer, you can demonstrate your interest and dedication to the position. Use your findings to tailor your responses and make a strong impression during the interview. Remember to also prepare for common questions and practice your responses to ensure you are ready for any curveballs that may come your way. With the right preparation and a little bit of research, you can ace your interview and land your dream job.

Developing a strong elevator pitch and responses to common interview questions

An elevator pitch is a brief, persuasive speech that you can use to introduce yourself, your experience, and your skills to potential employers or networking contacts. It's called an elevator pitch because it should be short enough to deliver during a brief elevator ride. Crafting a strong elevator pitch is essential for any job seeker because it can help you make a great first impression and stand out from other candidates.

When developing your elevator pitch, think about the key skills and experiences that you want to highlight. Focus on what makes you unique and what you can bring to the company. Keep in mind that your pitch should be tailored to the job you're applying for and the company culture.

To start, consider your overall career goals and how they align with the company's mission and values. This will help you craft a pitch that is relevant and meaningful to the employer. Be specific about the skills and experiences that you have that will make you an asset to the company. Remember to keep it brief and engaging, and practice delivering it with confidence.

In addition to your elevator pitch, it's important to prepare responses to common interview questions. While you can't predict every question that will be asked, there are some common ones that you can expect to hear. By preparing ahead of time, you can feel more confident and be better prepared to answer questions on the spot.

Some common interview questions include:

- Tell me about yourself.
- What are your strengths and weaknesses?
- Why do you want to work for this company?
- What is your greatest accomplishment?
- Can you describe a time when you overcame a challenge?
- How do you handle stress or difficult situations?
- What are your long-term career goals?
- What do you know about our company?

When preparing your responses, think about specific examples from your work experience that demonstrate your skills and abilities. Use the STAR method (Situation, Task, Action, Result) to structure your responses and provide concrete examples. Be honest and authentic, but also be mindful of the image you want to present to the employer.

Remember to also research the company and the interviewer ahead of time. Look up the company's mission statement, values, and recent news or developments. This will show the interviewer that you have a genuine interest in the company and are well-informed. You can also use this information to tailor your responses and ask thoughtful questions during the interview.

Finally, don't forget to practice. Rehearse your elevator pitch and responses to common interview questions with a friend or family member. This will help you feel more comfortable and confident during the actual interview. You can also record yourself and review the footage to see how you come across and identify areas for improvement.

In conclusion, developing a strong elevator pitch and preparing responses to common interview questions are essential for any job seeker. By tailoring your pitch and responses to the job and company, researching the company and interviewer, and practicing your delivery, you can make a great first impression and increase your chances of landing the job.

Chapter Seven

Navigating the Job Search Process

Applying to job postings and following up with employers

The job search process can be a long and arduous journey, but once you've found a job that's the right fit for you, the next step is to apply. While applying for a job may seem straightforward, it's important to approach it strategically to increase your chances of getting noticed and securing an interview.

The first step in applying to job postings is to carefully review the job description and requirements to ensure that you meet the necessary qualifications. If you do not have the required experience or education, it may not be worth your time to apply, as the employer is likely to receive a large number of applications from qualified candidates.

Once you have determined that you are a good fit for the position, it's time to tailor your resume and cover letter to the specific job. Use the keywords and phrases from the job description to ensure that your application stands out and is recognized by automated tracking systems used by many employers. Avoid generic cover letters or resumes that are not tailored to the specific job, as they are less likely to catch the attention of the hiring manager.

When submitting your application, be sure to follow the instructions provided by the employer. Some may require that you submit your materials through their online application system, while others may prefer email or regular mail. Pay close attention to any submission deadlines and ensure that you submit your materials in a timely manner.

After submitting your application, it's important to follow up with the employer to demonstrate your interest in the position and to ensure that your application was received. This can be done through a brief email or phone call, expressing your enthusiasm for the opportunity and asking if there is any additional information you can provide.

It's important to remember that the job search process can be competitive, and it may take some time to hear back from employers. While waiting to hear back, continue to search for other opportunities and refine your application materials to increase your chances of success.

If you are fortunate enough to receive an invitation for an interview, it's important to prepare thoroughly to make a good impression. Research the company and the industry, and be prepared to discuss your qualifications and how they align with the job requirements.

Another important aspect of the interview process is developing a strong elevator pitch and responses to common interview questions. An elevator pitch is a brief introduction that summarizes your qualifications and experience in a compelling way. This can be used at the beginning of the interview to make a positive first impression and to set the tone for the conversation.

It's also important to prepare responses to common interview questions, such as "What are your strengths and weaknesses?" and "Why are you interested in this job?" Practice your responses to these questions and be prepared to provide specific examples to support your answers.

During the interview, be sure to listen carefully to the interviewer's questions and respond thoughtfully. Ask clarifying questions if necessary, and use the opportunity to demonstrate your knowledge and enthusiasm for the job.

After the interview, be sure to follow up with a thank-you note or email to express your appreciation for the opportunity and to reiterate your interest in the position. This can help to keep you top of mind for the employer and increase your chances of being selected for the job.

Applying for job postings and following up with employers requires a strategic approach and attention to detail. Tailoring your application materials to the specific job, following submission instructions, and following up with the employer can increase your chances of getting noticed and securing an interview. Preparation is key when it comes to interviews, so be sure to research the company, develop a strong elevator pitch and responses to common interview questions, and follow up with a thank-you note after the interview. With these steps in mind, you can navigate the job search process with confidence and increase your chances of success.

Negotiating job offers and understanding compensation packages

Congratulations! You've aced the interview and received a job offer. Now comes the exciting and sometimes nerve-wracking part: negotiating the terms of the offer. Negotiating can be intimidating, but it's important to ensure that you are receiving fair compensation for your skills and experience.

Before you begin negotiating, it's important to understand the components of a compensation package. This package typically includes your salary, benefits, and any bonuses or incentives. Your salary is the most obvious and direct form of compensation, but benefits can also be very valuable. Benefits can include health insurance, retirement plans, paid time off, and other perks. It's important to evaluate the whole package and not just focus on your salary.

To start the negotiation process, you should first do your research. Find out what the average salary range is for the position in your industry and geographic location. You can use websites like Glassdoor and PayScale to get an idea of what other companies are offering for similar positions. This will give you a benchmark to use when negotiating your salary.

When negotiating your salary, it's important to be confident but also realistic. Don't ask for an amount that's far beyond what you would be happy with, but also don't accept an offer that's too low. Be prepared to back up your request with specific reasons why you deserve that salary, such as your experience, skills, and accomplishments.

It's also important to consider the benefits package. If the salary offer is lower than what you were hoping for, see if there's any flexibility in the benefits package. For example, you could ask for an extra week of paid vacation or a better health insurance plan. If the company is unable to negotiate the salary, you may be able to negotiate other aspects of the compensation package to make up for it.

Another important aspect of negotiating is timing. Don't wait too long to negotiate, but also don't rush into it right away. It's best to wait until you have a firm job offer before negotiating. Once you have an offer, it's appropriate to take a day or two to review it and prepare your counteroffer. Don't accept or reject the offer on the spot unless you are absolutely sure that it's the best option for you.

When negotiating, it's also important to maintain a positive and professional attitude. Remember that the goal is to find a mutually beneficial solution that works for both you and the employer. Be polite and respectful throughout the negotiation process, even if you don't end up getting everything you asked for. Keep in mind that you may be working with these people for a long time, so it's important to build a good relationship from the start.

Finally, once you have reached an agreement, make sure you get everything in writing. The offer letter should outline all the terms of your employment, including your salary, benefits, start date, and any other important details. Read it carefully and ask for clarification if anything is unclear.

Negotiating a job offer can be nerve-wracking, but it's an important part of the hiring process. Remember to do your research, be realistic and confident, consider the entire compensation package, time your negotiation appropriately, maintain a positive attitude, and get everything in writing. By following these tips, you'll be able to negotiate a fair and beneficial deal for both you and the employer.

Avoiding common pitfalls and mistakes in the job search process

The job search process can be a daunting and exhausting experience. From crafting the perfect resume and cover letter to navigating interviews and negotiating job offers, there are many potential pitfalls and mistakes that can hinder your success. In this article, we will explore some of the most common pitfalls and mistakes in the job search process, and provide tips and strategies to help you avoid them.

1. Applying to too many jobs at once
    One of the most common mistakes job seekers make is applying to too many jobs at once. While it may seem like a good strategy to cast a wide net and apply to as many jobs as possible, this can actually work against you. When you apply to too many jobs at once, it can be difficult to keep track of each application and tailor your approach to each specific opportunity. Instead, focus on a few key positions that are a good fit for your skills and experience, and take the time to craft personalized applications for each one.

2. Failing to tailor your resume and cover letter

Another common mistake job seekers make is using a generic resume and cover letter for every application. While it may save time in the short term, this approach can be detrimental in the long run. Employers can easily spot a generic application and may assume that you are not truly interested in their specific position. Instead, take the time to tailor your resume and cover letter to each job posting, highlighting the skills and experiences that are most relevant to the position.

3. Not following up after applying or interviewing
    Following up with an employer after applying or interviewing is a crucial step that many job seekers overlook. A well-timed follow-up email or phone call can demonstrate your continued interest in the position and help you stand out from other candidates. Be sure to thank the employer for their time and reiterate your enthusiasm for the position.

4. Over or underestimating your worth
    Negotiating salary and compensation can be a tricky business. On one hand, you want to be paid fairly for your skills and experience. On the other hand, you don't want to price yourself out of a job. It's important to do your research and understand the industry standards for compensation. This can help you negotiate a fair salary without over or underestimating your worth.

5. Being unprepared for interviews
    Preparing for interviews is essential to landing the job. This means researching the company and the position, developing a strong elevator pitch and responses to common interview questions, and practicing your

interview skills. Failing to prepare can make you appear uninterested or unprofessional, and can hurt your chances of getting the job.

6. Burning bridges with former employers
    It's important to maintain positive relationships with former employers, even if you left on less than ideal terms. Burning bridges can come back to haunt you later in your career, as employers may contact former colleagues for references or recommendations. Always strive to leave on good terms and maintain professional relationships, even if you don't plan on returning to the company.

The job search process can be full of potential pitfalls and mistakes. However, by taking the time to tailor your approach to each opportunity, following up with employers, negotiating salary and compensation, and being prepared for interviews, you can increase your chances of landing the job of your dreams. Remember to maintain positive relationships with former employers and to take a strategic approach to your job search. With these tips in mind, you can navigate the job search process with confidence and achieve your career goals.

Chapter Eight

Building Professional Skills

Developing skills that are in demand in your industry

In today's fast-paced and ever-changing job market, it's more important than ever to develop skills that are in demand in your industry. Whether you're just starting your career or looking to pivot to a new field, investing in your skills can help you stand out from the crowd and advance your career.

The first step in developing in-demand skills is to identify what those skills are. This can vary depending on your industry, but some examples of highly sought-after skills include:

1. Technical Skills: With the increasing digitization of many industries, technical skills such as coding, data analysis, and digital marketing are highly valued. Even if you're not in a tech-focused field, having some level of proficiency in these areas can make you a more attractive candidate.

2. Soft Skills: Soft skills, such as communication, teamwork, and problem-solving, are essential in any industry. Employers are looking for candidates who can

work effectively with others and who can adapt to changing circumstances.

3. Leadership Skills: Even if you're not in a management position, having strong leadership skills can make you a more valuable employee. This includes skills such as delegation, decision-making, and strategic planning.

Once you've identified the skills that are in demand in your industry, the next step is to start developing them. Here are some tips to help you get started:

1. Take courses or attend workshops: Many universities and community colleges offer courses and workshops that can help you develop new skills. Additionally, there are a variety of online resources available, such as Coursera and Udemy.

2. Participate in professional organizations: Joining a professional organization in your industry can provide opportunities to network and learn from others in your field. Many organizations offer training and development opportunities for their members.

3. Seek out mentorship: Finding a mentor in your industry can provide valuable guidance and insight into the skills and knowledge you need to succeed. Look for someone who has experience in your desired field and who is willing to share their expertise with you.

4. Take on new projects: Taking on new projects at work or volunteering for new assignments can help you develop new skills and demonstrate your ability to take initiative.

5. Stay up-to-date on industry trends: Keeping up with the latest trends and innovations in your industry can help you identify new skills to develop and stay ahead of the competition.

It's important to remember that developing in-demand skills is an ongoing process. The job market is constantly evolving, and what is in demand today may not be in demand tomorrow. Continuously seeking out new opportunities to learn and grow can help you stay ahead of the curve and position yourself as a valuable asset to any organization.

In addition to developing your skills, it's important to be able to articulate them effectively to potential employers. This is where having a strong elevator pitch comes in. An elevator pitch is a brief summary of your skills and experience that you can deliver in 30 seconds or less. It should be clear, concise, and highlight your unique strengths.

When crafting your elevator pitch, think about what sets you apart from other candidates. What unique skills or experiences do you bring to the table? What are your career goals and how do your skills align with those goals?

In addition to your elevator pitch, it's also important to be prepared for common interview questions related to your skills and experience. Some examples of questions you may be asked include:

1. What skills do you bring to this position?

2. How have you developed your skills in the past?

3. Can you give an example of a time when you had to use your skills to solve a problem?

4. How do your skills align with the needs of our organization?

Preparing thoughtful responses to these questions can help you showcase your skills and make a strong impression on potential employers.

Taking courses, attending workshops, and getting certified

To remain competitive and stand out in your field, it's essential to continue developing your skills and knowledge. Taking courses, attending workshops, and getting certified can all help you improve your skills, stay current with industry trends, and demonstrate to potential employers that you are committed to your profession.

Taking courses is a great way to acquire new skills or deepen your knowledge of a particular subject. Whether you're interested in learning about a new software program, mastering a new language, or delving into a specific field, there are courses available to meet your needs. Many colleges and universities offer continuing education courses, as do online learning platforms such as Coursera, Udemy, and LinkedIn Learning. These courses can be taken at your own pace, making it easy to fit them into your busy schedule.

Attending workshops is another effective way to develop your skills and knowledge. Workshops offer an opportunity to learn from experts in your field, network with other professionals, and get hands-on experience with new techniques or tools. Many industry conferences also include workshops as part of their programming, making them a great way to get the most out of your conference experience.

Getting certified is an excellent way to demonstrate your expertise and commitment to your profession. Many industries have certification programs that require passing an exam or completing a specific set of requirements. For example, if you're in the IT industry, you might consider getting certified in a specific programming language or platform. If you're in the healthcare industry, you might consider getting certified in a specific area of specialization. These certifications can help you stand out to potential employers and demonstrate your dedication to your profession.

One of the most significant advantages of taking courses, attending workshops, and getting certified is that they help you stay current with industry trends. In today's fast-paced job market, industries are constantly evolving, and new technologies and techniques are emerging all the time. By staying up-to-date with the latest developments in your field, you can remain competitive and increase your chances of landing your dream job.

In addition to helping you stay current, taking courses, attending workshops, and getting certified can also help you broaden your skill set. For example, if you're in the marketing industry, taking a course in graphic design or social media marketing can help you develop new skills that can be applied in your current role. Similarly, if you're in the IT industry, getting certified in a new programming language can help you expand your skill set and take on new challenges.

Finally, taking courses, attending workshops, and getting certified can help you build your professional network. By attending industry events and workshops, you can meet other professionals in your field and build relationships that can be valuable throughout your career. You never know when you might need a recommendation, advice, or help finding a job, so it's essential to build a strong network of professionals who can support you throughout your career.

Taking courses, attending workshops, and getting certified are all essential steps to developing your skills and staying ahead of the curve in your industry. By staying up-to-date with the latest developments in your field and broadening your skill set, you can increase your chances of landing your dream job and building a successful career. So, don't hesitate to invest in your professional development and take advantage of the many opportunities available to you!

Leveraging online resources and learning platforms to continue developing your skills

In today's rapidly changing job market, it is essential to continue developing your skills and staying up-to-date with the latest trends and technologies. Fortunately, there are a plethora of online resources and learning platforms that can help you achieve your career goals. In this article, we'll explore some of the best ways to leverage these resources and continue developing your skills.

First and foremost, online courses are a great way to learn new skills and brush up on existing ones. There are many reputable platforms that offer online courses, such as Udemy, Coursera, and edX. These platforms offer courses in a wide variety of subjects, from programming and data science to marketing and project management.

One of the benefits of online courses is that they are often self-paced, meaning you can learn at your own pace and on your own schedule. This is especially beneficial for those who work full-time or have other commitments that make attending in-person classes difficult. Additionally, many courses offer certificates of completion, which can be a valuable addition to your resume.

In addition to online courses, there are also many workshops and webinars that you can attend to further develop your skills. These can be hosted by industry leaders or companies in your field, and often cover specific topics or technologies. Attending these events can not only help you learn new skills, but also provide opportunities to network with others in your industry.

Another way to leverage online resources is to join online communities or forums related to your field. These communities can provide a wealth of knowledge and resources, as well as opportunities to connect with others in your industry. For example, if you're a web developer, joining online communities like Stack Overflow or GitHub can help you stay up-to-date with the latest technologies and connect with other developers.

There are also many free resources available online, such as YouTube tutorials and blog posts. While these may not be as comprehensive as online courses or workshops, they can still be a valuable way to learn new skills or brush up on existing ones. Many experts in various fields share their knowledge and insights for free on their personal blogs or social media accounts, so it's worth seeking out these resources.

In addition to online resources, there are also many certifications that you can pursue to demonstrate your expertise in a particular area. These certifications can be valuable additions to your resume and can help you stand out in a crowded job market. For example, if you're in the IT field, certifications like CompTIA A+ or Cisco Certified Network Associate (CCNA) can demonstrate your proficiency in hardware or networking.

Lastly, it's worth noting that developing your skills doesn't necessarily mean learning new technologies or tools. Soft skills, such as communication, teamwork, and leadership, are also highly valued in the workplace. There are many resources available online to help you improve these skills, such as online courses and webinars focused on communication or leadership.

There are many ways to leverage online resources and learning platforms to continue developing your skills. From online courses and workshops to certifications and online communities, there are many opportunities to learn and grow in your career. By staying up-to-date with the latest trends and technologies, you can position yourself for success in the job market and achieve your career goals.

Chapter Nine

Excelling in Your Current Job

Building strong relationships with colleagues and managers

As the saying goes, "no man is an island," and this rings especially true in the workplace. Building strong relationships with colleagues and managers is crucial to not only surviving, but thriving in a professional setting. In fact, studies have shown that positive workplace relationships lead to increased job satisfaction, better job performance, and even lower rates of absenteeism.

So, how can you build strong relationships with your colleagues and managers? Here are some tips to help you get started:

1. Be a good listener: When your colleagues or manager is speaking, give them your full attention. Don't interrupt or try to multitask while they are talking. Show genuine interest in what they are saying and respond appropriately. By being a good listener, you demonstrate that you value their input and ideas.

2. Be reliable: Show up to meetings on time, meet deadlines, and follow through on your commitments.

Your colleagues and manager will appreciate that they can count on you to do what you say you will do.

3. Collaborate: Be open to collaborating with your colleagues on projects. When you work together, you can often come up with better solutions and ideas than you would on your own. Plus, by working collaboratively, you show that you are a team player and that you value others' contributions.

4. Offer help: If you see a colleague struggling with a task, offer to help. This not only helps your colleague, but it also shows that you are a team player who is willing to pitch in when needed.

5. Be positive: No one wants to work with someone who is negative or constantly complaining. Instead, try to maintain a positive attitude and focus on finding solutions rather than dwelling on problems.

6. Communicate effectively: Good communication is key to building strong relationships in the workplace. Be clear and concise in your communications, and make sure you are communicating in a way that works for the person you are speaking with.

7. Show appreciation: When a colleague or manager does something that you appreciate, let them know. A simple thank you can go a long way in building strong relationships.

8. Get to know your colleagues: Take the time to get to know your colleagues as people, not just as coworkers. Ask them about their interests outside of work, and look for commonalities that you can build on.

9. Respect boundaries: While it's important to build strong relationships with your colleagues and manager, it's also important to respect their boundaries. If someone doesn't want to talk about a particular topic, respect their wishes.

10. Be yourself: Finally, be yourself. Authenticity is key to building strong relationships. Don't try to be someone you're not in order to fit in or impress others.

Building strong relationships with colleagues and managers takes time and effort, but the payoff is well worth it. By following these tips, you can create a positive work environment where everyone feels valued and supported.

Communicating effectively and managing your workload

In today's fast-paced work environment, communication and time management skills are crucial for career success. Regardless of the industry or position, effective communication is essential to building strong relationships with colleagues and clients, while managing workload efficiently ensures productivity and job satisfaction. In this article, we will discuss some tips for communicating effectively and managing your workload.

Effective communication is the foundation of any successful workplace. It is important to be clear, concise, and timely in your communication. Whether it is through email, phone, or face-to-face conversation, always ensure that your message is conveyed clearly and effectively. When communicating through email, use proper grammar and spelling, and avoid using jargon or slang. Be respectful and courteous, and remember to proofread your message before sending it.

When communicating with colleagues or clients face-to-face, always be present and engaged. Pay attention to their body language and tone of voice, and respond appropriately. Practice active listening, which involves not only hearing what the other person is saying but also acknowledging and understanding their message. Ask questions to clarify any uncertainties, and avoid interrupting or talking over others.

In addition to effective communication, managing workload efficiently is critical to job success. Time management involves setting priorities, delegating tasks, and allocating time to each task effectively. To manage your workload, start by creating a to-do list, including all tasks that need to be completed. Prioritize the tasks by their level of importance, and allocate time for each task based on its level of urgency.

One way to manage workload effectively is to delegate tasks to others. Delegating tasks to colleagues or team members not only helps you manage your workload but also encourages teamwork and collaboration. When delegating tasks, make sure to communicate clearly what is expected of the person, set a deadline, and offer support and resources if needed.

Another important aspect of workload management is setting boundaries. It is easy to fall into the trap of overworking, which can lead to burnout and decreased productivity. Setting boundaries by scheduling breaks and avoiding work during non-work hours can help prevent burnout and ensure that you are able to manage your workload efficiently.

In addition to these tips, there are various tools and resources available to help you communicate effectively and manage your workload efficiently. For example, project management software can help you prioritize and delegate tasks, while time-tracking tools can help you monitor your work hours and ensure that you are meeting deadlines. Additionally, there are numerous online courses and training programs available that can help you develop effective communication and time management skills.

In conclusion, effective communication and workload management skills are essential for career success. By practicing active listening, clear communication, prioritization, delegation, and setting boundaries, you can effectively manage your workload and communicate with colleagues and clients in a productive and efficient manner. Remember to utilize the various tools and resources available to you to enhance your skills and improve your overall performance in the workplace.

Finding opportunities for growth and advancement in your current role

As you settle into your job, you may start to wonder about opportunities for growth and advancement within your current role. Perhaps you are interested in taking on more responsibilities, learning new skills, or even moving up the career ladder. Whatever your aspirations may be, it is important to approach this process with intention and strategy.

First and foremost, it is important to have a clear understanding of the expectations and requirements for your current role. Make sure you have a good grasp of your job duties and are meeting or exceeding expectations. This will lay a strong foundation for any future growth opportunities.

Next, consider the skills and knowledge that are necessary for advancement within your industry. Are there certain certifications or trainings that are highly valued? Do you need to develop expertise in a particular area? Take the time to research and identify these skills, and then seek out opportunities to acquire them. This could include attending conferences, enrolling in classes, or even asking your manager for additional training or mentoring.

Networking is also an important aspect of finding opportunities for growth and advancement. Build relationships with colleagues and managers in your department, as well as with those in other areas of the organization. Attend company events and social gatherings, and be sure to follow up with new connections afterward. Consider joining professional associations or industry groups to expand your network even further.

Don't be afraid to have open and honest conversations with your manager about your career goals and aspirations. Your manager can provide valuable insight and guidance on the skills and experiences necessary for advancement within your organization. Ask for feedback on your performance, and work together to identify opportunities for growth and development.

Another important aspect of finding opportunities for growth is to be open to taking on new challenges and responsibilities. Volunteer for special projects or cross-functional teams, and seek out opportunities to collaborate with colleagues in other departments. This will not only help you to develop new skills, but it will also help you to build relationships and gain visibility within the organization.

It's important to remember that opportunities for growth and advancement may not always come in the form of a promotion or new job title. Look for ways to expand your role and take on additional responsibilities within your current position. This could include leading a team, spearheading a new initiative, or taking on a leadership role in a professional association.

Finally, it is important to stay up-to-date with industry trends and developments. This could include attending conferences, reading industry publications, or participating in online forums and discussion groups. By staying informed, you will be better positioned to identify new opportunities for growth and advancement as they arise.

In summary, finding opportunities for growth and advancement within your current role requires a combination of strategy, intention, and action. Take the time to understand the expectations and requirements for your current position, identify the skills and knowledge necessary for advancement, and build strong relationships with colleagues and managers. Be open to taking on new challenges and responsibilities, and stay informed about industry trends and developments. With a proactive and intentional approach, you can create a pathway to professional growth and success.

Chapter Ten

Managing Your Finances

Understanding the financial implications of building a career

Building a career is an exciting and challenging journey that requires a great deal of effort and dedication. However, it is important to understand the financial implications of building a career, especially since it can impact your life in many ways.

One of the most significant financial implications of building a career is the need to invest in your education and training. This may involve going to college or attending courses, workshops, and certification programs. These investments can be costly, and it is important to plan ahead and budget accordingly.

Another important factor to consider is the impact that your career choice will have on your earning potential. While some careers offer high salaries, others may pay less but offer other benefits such as flexibility, job security, or opportunities for growth and advancement. It is important to weigh the financial benefits and drawbacks of each career choice and determine what is most important to you.

In addition to earning potential, it is also important to consider the cost of living in the areas where you are considering building your career. Different regions may have different costs of living, and you may need to adjust your expectations and lifestyle accordingly. For example, living in a city with a high cost of living may require you to take on additional work or seek out higher-paying jobs.

Another financial consideration is the need to build an emergency fund to prepare for unexpected expenses such as job loss, illness, or major repairs. It is recommended to have at least three to six months of living expenses saved in an emergency fund to help you weather any financial storms that may come your way.

Investing in a retirement account is also an important financial consideration when building a career. Many employers offer retirement plans such as 401(k)s or pensions, and it is important to take advantage of these opportunities to save for your future. Additionally, you may want to consider opening an individual retirement account (IRA) or investing in other financial vehicles to help grow your savings over time.

It is also important to consider the financial implications of job changes and career transitions. Switching careers may require additional education or training, which can be costly. Additionally, changing jobs may mean a temporary decrease in income or benefits, which can impact your financial stability. It is important to consider these factors and plan ahead to ensure a smooth transition.

Finally, it is important to consider the long-term financial implications of building a career. This may include setting financial goals such as paying off debt, saving for a down payment on a home, or investing in a long-term savings plan. It may also involve creating a budget to manage your expenses and stay on track with your financial goals.

Building a career is a rewarding and exciting journey, but it is important to understand the financial implications of this process. By investing in education and training, considering earning potential and cost of living, building an emergency fund, saving for retirement, and planning for job changes and transitions, you can set yourself up for financial success and security.

Creating a budget and managing your expenses

Money management can be a daunting task, but it is an essential skill to develop in order to achieve financial stability and achieve your goals. One of the most important aspects of managing your finances is creating and sticking to a budget. A budget is essentially a plan that outlines your income and expenses, allowing you to see where your money is going and make adjustments accordingly.

To start creating a budget, you need to first track your income and expenses. This can be done manually or by using a budgeting app or software. Start by listing all of your sources of income, such as your salary or any side hustles you have. Then, list all of your expenses, including rent or mortgage payments, utilities, food, transportation, entertainment, and any other recurring expenses.

Once you have a clear picture of your income and expenses, it's time to create a budget that works for you. Start by prioritizing your expenses, making sure to cover the essentials first. This means ensuring that you have enough money to pay for housing, food, transportation, and other necessary expenses. From there, you can allocate funds to other categories such as entertainment and savings.

It's important to note that your budget is not set in stone and can be adjusted as needed. If you find that you are overspending in certain categories, it may be necessary to cut back in other areas or look for ways to increase your income. This can involve finding ways to earn more money, such as taking on a part-time job or starting a side business.

In addition to creating a budget, it's important to practice good habits when it comes to managing your expenses. This includes being mindful of your spending, avoiding impulse purchases, and finding ways to save money on everyday expenses. This can involve using coupons or shopping during sales, buying generic or store-brand products, and avoiding unnecessary expenses like dining out or subscription services that you don't use.

Another important aspect of managing your finances is staying organized. This means keeping track of your bills and payments, and setting up automatic payments whenever possible to avoid late fees or missed payments. It also involves regularly checking your credit score and report to ensure that everything is accurate and up-to-date.

Managing your expenses and creating a budget can seem overwhelming at first, but it's a skill that can be developed with practice and dedication. By taking the time to track your income and expenses, prioritize your spending, and practice good habits, you can gain control over your finances and work towards achieving your goals. Whether you're saving for a big purchase or planning for your future, a solid financial foundation is key to achieving success.

Investing in your future and building long-term financial stability

When it comes to building long-term financial stability, investing in your future is key. Whether you're just starting out in your career or you've been working for years, there are steps you can take to ensure that you're on track for a secure financial future.

One of the most important things you can do is to start saving and investing as early as possible. This doesn't have to mean investing large amounts of money – even small, regular contributions to a retirement account or other investment vehicle can add up over time. In fact, the earlier you start investing, the more time your money has to grow through the power of compound interest.

Another key step in building financial stability is to minimize your debt. While some types of debt – like a mortgage or student loans – can be necessary, high-interest credit card debt can be a major drain on your finances. If you have credit card debt, consider taking steps to pay it off as quickly as possible, such as making larger payments each month or consolidating your debt into a lower-interest loan.

In addition to saving and investing, it's important to be strategic about your career choices. While higher-paying jobs may be tempting, it's important to consider factors like job security, benefits, and opportunities for advancement when deciding which job to take. Additionally, investing in your education and skills can help you stay competitive in the job market and increase your earning potential over time.

Another way to build long-term financial stability is to create a comprehensive financial plan. This should include setting specific goals for savings and investing, as well as a budget for your monthly expenses. You may also want to work with a financial advisor to help you navigate more complex financial issues, like tax planning or estate planning.

Finally, it's important to think about long-term financial stability in terms of not just your own financial situation, but also the wider economic landscape. This means staying informed about economic trends and developments, as well as being prepared for unexpected events like recessions or market downturns. It may also mean taking steps to contribute to the broader economic well-being, such as supporting policies that promote economic growth and stability.

Ultimately, building long-term financial stability requires a combination of smart financial choices, careful planning, and a willingness to adapt to changing circumstances. By taking steps to save and invest, minimize debt, invest in your education and skills, and create a comprehensive financial plan, you can set yourself up for a secure financial future. And by staying informed about economic trends and contributing to the broader economic well-being, you can help ensure that your financial stability is part of a larger, sustainable economic system.

Chapter Eleven

Maintaining Work-Life Balance

Prioritizing self-care and wellness

Self-care and wellness are essential aspects of living a happy and fulfilling life. It is imperative that we prioritize these aspects of our lives in today's fast-paced world, where we are constantly running around, trying to meet deadlines, and juggling multiple responsibilities. It can be challenging to take a step back and prioritize our health and well-being, but it is crucial to ensure that we can continue to function at our best and maintain a positive outlook on life.

Self-care and wellness are not just about taking bubble baths or going on luxurious vacations, although those things can certainly help. It is about making a conscious effort to take care of ourselves physically, emotionally, and mentally. It means carving out time for ourselves, setting boundaries, and recognizing when we need to take a break and recharge.

Physical self-care can include activities such as getting enough sleep, eating healthy and nutritious food, and exercising regularly. We often hear that we need to get enough sleep, but it can be challenging to prioritize it when we have so many things on our to-do lists. However, sleep is crucial for our bodies to function correctly, and without it, we can feel fatigued, irritable, and unable to concentrate. Eating a balanced and healthy diet can also have a significant impact on our physical health. Fueling our bodies with the right nutrients can help us maintain a healthy weight, lower our risk of developing chronic illnesses, and boost our mood and energy levels. Regular exercise is also essential for our physical well-being. It can help us maintain a healthy weight, improve our cardiovascular health, and reduce our risk of developing chronic illnesses such as diabetes and heart disease.

Emotional self-care is also important. This can include activities such as spending time with loved ones, engaging in hobbies, practicing mindfulness or meditation, and seeking professional help if needed. Our emotional well-being is just as important as our physical health, and neglecting it can have serious consequences. Spending time with loved ones and engaging in activities that bring us joy can help us reduce stress and anxiety, and improve our overall mood. Practicing mindfulness or meditation can also help us reduce stress and improve our mental well-being. It can help us become more present in the moment, and reduce the constant chatter in our minds.

Mental self-care is equally important. It involves taking care of our mental health, which can be just as important as our physical health. This can include activities such as seeking therapy, practicing stress-reducing techniques, and avoiding negative self-talk. Our mental health can have a significant impact on our overall well-being, and neglecting it can lead to serious consequences. Seeking therapy or professional help when needed can be incredibly beneficial for our mental health, and can help us work through any issues or challenges we may be facing. Practicing stress-reducing techniques such as deep breathing or yoga can also help us manage our stress levels and improve our mental health.

Prioritizing self-care and wellness may seem like an indulgence, but it is essential for our overall well-being. It can help us become more productive, focused, and fulfilled, and allow us to maintain a positive outlook on life. It is important to remember that self-care and wellness are not selfish acts, but necessary ones. Taking care of ourselves allows us to take care of those around us, and to be the best versions of ourselves. So, let us prioritize self-care and wellness in our daily lives, and watch as it transforms our overall well-being.

Finding ways to de-stress and recharge outside of work

As we navigate the demands and stresses of modern life, it can be challenging to find ways to unwind and recharge outside of work. With the constant barrage of emails, meetings, and deadlines, it can feel like we never truly disconnect from our work, leaving us feeling drained and depleted. That's why it's crucial to prioritize self-care and find healthy ways to de-stress and recharge outside of the office.

One of the most effective ways to de-stress is by engaging in physical activity. Whether it's a brisk walk in nature, a yoga class, or a game of pickup basketball, exercise has been shown to reduce stress and boost mood. When we engage in physical activity, our bodies release endorphins, which are natural mood boosters that help us feel happier and more relaxed. Additionally, exercise can help us feel more energized and focused, which can help us be more productive when we return to work.

Another way to de-stress and recharge is by engaging in creative activities. Whether it's painting, writing, or playing music, creative pursuits allow us to express ourselves and tap into our imaginations, which can be incredibly rejuvenating. When we engage in creative activities, we give our minds a break from the stresses of work and allow ourselves to explore new ideas and perspectives.

Spending time in nature is another powerful way to de-stress and recharge. Whether it's taking a hike, going for a swim, or simply sitting outside and enjoying the fresh air, being in nature has been shown to reduce stress and improve overall well-being. When we spend time in nature, we allow ourselves to connect with something larger than ourselves, which can help us feel more grounded and centered.

Connecting with loved ones is another crucial way to de-stress and recharge. Whether it's spending time with family, catching up with old friends, or making new connections, socializing can help us feel more connected and supported. When we connect with others, we feel a sense of belonging and community, which can be incredibly nourishing for our well-being.

Finally, it's important to prioritize rest and relaxation. In our fast-paced world, it can be tempting to push ourselves to the limit, but rest is crucial for our physical and emotional health. Whether it's taking a nap, reading a book, or simply sitting in silence, allowing ourselves to rest and recharge is essential for our overall well-being.

Finding ways to de-stress and recharge outside of work is crucial for our well-being and overall happiness. By prioritizing self-care and engaging in activities that bring us joy and relaxation, we can create a more balanced and fulfilling life. So, whether it's going for a walk in nature, spending time with loved ones, or simply taking a nap, make sure to take the time to recharge and care for yourself. After all, you deserve it.

Balancing career goals with personal responsibilities and interests

As we strive to achieve our career goals and pursue success in our professional lives, it can be all too easy to lose sight of the other important aspects of our lives. Personal responsibilities and interests are often pushed to the side in the relentless pursuit of career advancement. However, maintaining a healthy work-life balance is essential to our overall well-being and success in all areas of our lives.

Balancing career goals with personal responsibilities and interests can be challenging, but it is not impossible. It requires a careful and intentional approach to managing our time and energy. Here are some tips for finding balance and living a fulfilling life both inside and outside of the workplace.

First and foremost, it's important to prioritize the things that matter most to you. Take some time to reflect on what brings you joy and fulfillment outside of work. Whether it's spending time with family and friends, pursuing a hobby, or volunteering in your community, make sure to carve out time for these activities on a regular basis. By making time for the things that matter most, you'll be better equipped to handle the stresses of your career and feel more fulfilled overall.

Another important aspect of balancing career goals with personal responsibilities and interests is setting boundaries. It can be all too easy to let work bleed into our personal lives, but it's important to establish clear boundaries between the two. This might mean setting aside specific times of the day or week for work-related tasks, or even disconnecting entirely from work emails and notifications during non-work hours. By creating clear boundaries between work and personal time, you'll be able to fully engage in both areas of your life without feeling overwhelmed or burnt out.

It's also important to remember that self-care is an essential part of maintaining balance in our lives. Taking care of our physical, mental, and emotional health is crucial to our overall well-being and success in all areas of our lives. Make sure to prioritize activities that help you relax and recharge, whether it's getting enough sleep, exercising regularly, or taking time to meditate or practice mindfulness. By taking care of yourself, you'll be better equipped to handle the demands of your career and personal life.

In addition to prioritizing self-care, it's also important to cultivate a strong support system. Surround yourself with people who uplift and support you in your career goals, but also understand the importance of your personal responsibilities and interests. Make time for meaningful connections with family and friends, and seek out mentors and colleagues who can provide guidance and support in your career. By cultivating a strong support system, you'll be better equipped to navigate the challenges and stresses of both your professional and personal life.

Finally, it's important to remember that balance is not a static state, but rather an ongoing process. As our lives and careers evolve, our priorities and responsibilities will shift, and it's important to be flexible and adapt accordingly. Don't be afraid to reassess your priorities and make changes as needed to ensure that you're living a balanced and fulfilling life.

Balancing career goals with personal responsibilities and interests is essential to living a fulfilling life. By prioritizing the things that matter most, setting clear boundaries, prioritizing self-care, cultivating a strong support system, and remaining flexible, we can achieve balance and success in all areas of our lives. So go forth and pursue your career goals, but remember to take care of yourself and the other important aspects of your life along the way.

Chapter Twelve

Overcoming Career Challenges

Dealing with setbacks and failures

Life is not always a bed of roses. We all experience setbacks and failures in our journey, whether it's in our personal or professional lives. However, the way we handle these challenges can make all the difference in our future success. Dealing with setbacks and failures is an important skill to master if we want to achieve our goals and reach our full potential.

One of the first things to remember when dealing with setbacks and failures is that it's a natural part of life. No one is immune to experiencing failures or setbacks, no matter how successful they may appear to be. It's important to understand that we all have our share of failures and setbacks, and that they are simply part of the learning process.

When we face setbacks and failures, it's easy to get discouraged and lose motivation. However, it's important to remember that setbacks and failures can actually be valuable learning experiences. When we fail, we have the opportunity to reflect on what went wrong and why, and to make adjustments for the future. It's essential to use failures and setbacks as opportunities for growth and learning.

One way to deal with setbacks and failures is to stay positive and focus on the bigger picture. It's easy to get bogged down in the details of what went wrong, but it's important to keep our eyes on the ultimate goal. By maintaining a positive attitude and focusing on the bigger picture, we can stay motivated and keep moving forward.

Another important step in dealing with setbacks and failures is to seek support from others. It can be helpful to talk to friends, family, or colleagues about our experiences and seek their advice and guidance. Often, the support of others can help us stay positive and motivated during difficult times.

It's also important to take care of ourselves physically and emotionally when dealing with setbacks and failures. Exercise, healthy eating, and getting enough sleep can help us manage stress and maintain a positive outlook. We should also make time for activities that we enjoy, such as hobbies or spending time with loved ones. Taking care of ourselves can help us bounce back from setbacks and failures more quickly and effectively.

In addition, it's important to learn from our setbacks and failures and use them as opportunities to improve. We should take time to reflect on what went wrong and why, and consider how we can make adjustments for the future. This might involve seeking additional training or education, or simply making changes to our approach or mindset.

Finally, it's important to stay persistent and keep trying, even in the face of setbacks and failures. Success rarely comes easily, and setbacks and failures are simply part of the journey. It's essential to keep pushing forward, even when things get tough. By staying persistent and resilient, we can overcome setbacks and failures and ultimately achieve our goals.

Setbacks and failures are an inevitable part of life, but they don't have to hold us back. By staying positive, seeking support, taking care of ourselves, learning from our experiences, and staying persistent, we can overcome setbacks and failures and ultimately achieve success. Remember, it's not about avoiding failures and setbacks, but rather how we handle them that determines our future success.

Building resilience and bouncing back from difficult situations

Life can be unpredictable, and sometimes, even the most well-laid plans can go awry. You may encounter unexpected setbacks, face difficult challenges, or experience failures that leave you feeling defeated and demotivated. However, the key to success lies not in avoiding these obstacles but in how you respond to them.

Resilience is the ability to bounce back from difficult situations and to overcome adversity. It's a skill that can be developed and strengthened over time, and it's essential for building a successful career and a fulfilling life.

One of the first steps to building resilience is to develop a growth mindset. A growth mindset is the belief that your abilities and talents can be developed through hard work, dedication, and learning from your mistakes. This mindset helps you see setbacks and failures as opportunities for growth and development, rather than as indicators of your worth or potential.

Another important aspect of building resilience is to take care of yourself physically, mentally, and emotionally. This includes getting enough sleep, eating a healthy diet, exercising regularly, and practicing mindfulness and self-care activities. When you're well-rested and balanced, you're better able to cope with stress and challenges.

It's also important to cultivate a strong support system of family, friends, and colleagues. Surrounding yourself with positive and supportive people can help you stay motivated and encouraged during difficult times. Don't be afraid to ask for help or seek out support when you need it.

Another key to building resilience is to learn from your failures and setbacks. Rather than dwelling on your mistakes or beating yourself up for them, use them as opportunities for growth and development. Take the time to reflect on what went wrong, what you could have done differently, and what you can learn from the experience.

In addition, it's important to stay flexible and adaptable in the face of change and uncertainty. Be willing to pivot and adjust your plans as needed, and embrace new opportunities and challenges with an open mind and a willingness to learn.

Finally, it's important to stay motivated and focused on your goals, even when faced with setbacks or obstacles. Keep your long-term vision in mind, and use your setbacks as fuel to drive you forward. Use positive affirmations and visualization techniques to stay focused and motivated, and celebrate small wins along the way.

Building resilience takes time and effort, but it's a critical skill for navigating life's ups and downs. By developing a growth mindset, taking care of yourself physically and emotionally, cultivating a strong support system, learning from your failures, staying flexible and adaptable, and staying motivated and focused on your goals, you can bounce back from difficult situations and overcome adversity to achieve success in your career and in life.

Finding support and resources to help you overcome obstacles

Life is full of ups and downs, and sometimes, despite our best efforts, we encounter obstacles that seem impossible to overcome. Whether it's a personal setback, a professional challenge, or a health issue, it's essential to have a support system in place to help us navigate these difficult times.

When we are facing adversity, it can be easy to feel alone and isolated. It's essential to remember that we are not alone in our struggles and that there are people and resources available to help us overcome obstacles. The first step in finding support is to reach out to those around us, whether it's family, friends, or colleagues. Talking about our challenges and sharing our feelings can be an incredibly powerful way to gain perspective and get the support we need.

In addition to reaching out to those around us, there are also many resources available that can help us overcome obstacles. From support groups to therapy, there are many options to choose from depending on our needs and preferences.

One resource that can be incredibly helpful in times of need is a support group. Support groups bring together people who are facing similar challenges, providing a safe space to share experiences and offer mutual support. There are support groups available for a wide range of issues, from addiction to grief to chronic illness, and many more. Attending a support group can be a powerful way to connect with others who are going through similar struggles and gain valuable insights into how to overcome obstacles.

Another resource that can be helpful is therapy. Therapy provides a safe and confidential space to explore our thoughts, feelings, and behaviors with the guidance of a trained professional. A therapist can help us identify patterns and beliefs that may be holding us back and provide tools and strategies to overcome obstacles. There are many different types of therapy available, from cognitive-behavioral therapy to mindfulness-based therapy, and finding the right fit for our needs can be a powerful step towards overcoming obstacles.

In addition to support groups and therapy, there are also many self-help resources available that can help us overcome obstacles. From books to podcasts to online courses, there are many resources available that can provide insights and strategies to help us build resilience and overcome challenges. The key is to find resources that resonate with our needs and preferences and to commit to the work of implementing the strategies we learn.

It's important to remember that finding support and resources is not a sign of weakness, but rather a sign of strength. It takes courage to reach out and ask for help, and it's essential to recognize that we all need support from time to time. Whether it's a listening ear or a professional resource, finding the right support can make all the difference in our ability to overcome obstacles and thrive in our personal and professional lives.

Finding support and resources to help us overcome obstacles is an essential part of building resilience and thriving in our lives. Whether we reach out to those around us, attend a support group, seek therapy, or explore self-help resources, the key is to take action and commit to the work of overcoming challenges. It's not always easy, but with the right support and resources, we can build resilience, bounce back from difficult situations, and continue to grow and thrive in our lives.

Chapter Thirteen

Embracing Change and Innovation

Staying up-to-date with industry trends and advancements

In today's fast-paced and ever-changing world, staying up-to-date with industry trends and advancements is essential for anyone looking to build a successful career. Whether you are a seasoned professional or just starting out, it is important to keep abreast of new technologies, emerging markets, and shifting consumer preferences in your field.

One way to stay informed is by attending industry conferences and events. These gatherings provide an opportunity to hear from experts in your field, network with peers, and gain insights into the latest trends and innovations. Many conferences also offer workshops and training sessions that can help you develop new skills and stay ahead of the curve.

In addition to attending events, reading industry publications and blogs is another great way to stay up-to-date. There are a wealth of online resources available, from trade publications to industry blogs, that provide in-depth analysis and commentary on the latest developments in your field. By following these sources, you can stay informed about emerging trends, new products and services, and key players in your industry.

Another effective strategy for staying up-to-date is by leveraging online learning platforms. Many websites offer courses and tutorials on a range of topics, from programming languages to marketing strategies. By taking advantage of these resources, you can acquire new skills and deepen your understanding of key concepts in your field. Some platforms also offer certifications that can help you stand out to potential employers and clients.

Another important aspect of staying up-to-date is keeping an eye on emerging technologies and disruptive innovations. Whether you work in healthcare, finance, or technology, new technologies are constantly reshaping the landscape of nearly every industry. By keeping a watchful eye on emerging trends, you can position yourself as a thought leader and stay ahead of the competition.

Of course, staying up-to-date is not just about acquiring knowledge. It is also about developing a mindset of curiosity and continuous learning. By approaching your work with a sense of curiosity and a willingness to explore new ideas, you can stay energized and engaged even in the face of uncertainty and change.

At the same time, it is important to be discerning about the information you consume. With so much content available online, it can be difficult to separate valuable insights from noise. To avoid getting bogged down by irrelevant information, focus on sources that are reputable and well-regarded in your industry. Look for content that is well-researched, well-written, and offers a unique perspective on the latest trends and developments.

Finally, it is important to stay connected to others in your field. By networking with peers and colleagues, you can gain valuable insights into the latest trends and developments, as well as potential career opportunities. Networking can also provide emotional support and encouragement, particularly during times of uncertainty or change.

Staying up-to-date with industry trends and advancements is essential for anyone looking to build a successful career. By attending events, reading industry publications and blogs, leveraging online learning platforms, and staying connected to others in your field, you can stay informed, develop new skills, and position yourself as a thought leader in your industry.

Embracing change and adapting to new technologies and work environments

It is very important to be able to adapt and accept changes in our time. This is especially true when it comes to technology and the work environment, which is constantly evolving and changing at an unprecedented rate.

For many of us, change can be intimidating, and adapting to new technologies and work environments can seem overwhelming. However, it's important to remember that change is inevitable, and by embracing it, we can open up new opportunities and possibilities for personal and professional growth.

One of the keys to successfully adapting to new technologies and work environments is to stay curious and open-minded. This means being willing to explore new tools, methods, and approaches, even if they are unfamiliar or uncomfortable at first. By keeping an open mind, we can discover new ways of doing things and unlock new possibilities for innovation and creativity.

Another important aspect of adapting to change is to seek out learning opportunities. This can mean taking classes, attending workshops or seminars, or even just reading books or articles about new technologies and approaches. By investing in our own education and development, we can stay up-to-date with the latest trends and advancements and be better prepared to adapt to new environments and challenges.

Networking and building relationships with others in our industry can also be a valuable way to stay informed and adaptable. By connecting with peers and experts in our field, we can learn from their experiences and insights, and stay on top of new developments and trends. Networking can also provide valuable opportunities for collaboration and partnership, which can help us to adapt more quickly and effectively to change.

When it comes to adapting to new work environments, it's important to be flexible and adaptable. This means being willing to take on new roles and responsibilities, and to work in different environments and with different people. It also means being able to manage our own stress levels and emotions, and to maintain a positive and proactive attitude, even in the face of uncertainty or adversity.

Finally, it's important to remember that change can be a positive thing. By embracing new technologies and work environments, we can open up new opportunities and possibilities for personal and professional growth. We can learn new skills, develop new interests, and discover new passions. And by adapting to change, we can become more resilient, more creative, and more adaptable, which can help us to thrive in the face of uncertainty and challenge.

Embracing change and adapting to new technologies and work environments is essential in today's rapidly evolving world. By staying curious, seeking out learning opportunities, networking with peers and experts, and being flexible and adaptable, we can stay on top of new trends and advancements, and unlock new opportunities for personal and professional growth. And by maintaining a positive and proactive attitude, we can navigate change with confidence and resilience, and emerge stronger and more adaptable than ever before.

Finding ways to innovate and stand out in your field

In today's rapidly changing world, it is important to not only keep up with industry trends and advancements but to also find ways to innovate and stand out in your field. The ability to think creatively and come up with new ideas can help you stay ahead of the competition and achieve success in your career.

One way to innovate is to constantly challenge yourself to think outside the box. This means taking risks and trying new things, even if they may not seem like the most obvious or conventional approach. It can be tempting to stick with what has worked in the past, but in order to truly innovate, you must be willing to take a chance and explore new ideas.

Another key to innovation is collaboration. Working with others who have different perspectives and skill sets can help you generate fresh ideas and solutions to complex problems. Whether it's brainstorming with colleagues or partnering with other organizations, collaboration can lead to exciting new opportunities and help you stand out in your field.

In addition to collaboration, it's also important to stay on top of emerging technologies and trends in your industry. This can involve attending conferences and workshops, reading industry publications, and participating in online communities and forums. By staying up-to-date with the latest developments in your field, you can identify new opportunities and stay ahead of the curve.

Another way to stand out is to focus on developing unique skills or expertise. This could involve pursuing additional education or training, or seeking out opportunities to gain hands-on experience in areas that are in demand. By specializing in a particular area or developing a unique skill set, you can set yourself apart from others in your field and position yourself for success.

Networking is another important aspect of standing out in your field. Building relationships with colleagues, industry leaders, and potential clients can open doors to new opportunities and help you gain visibility within your industry. Whether it's attending industry events, participating in online communities, or simply reaching out to people you admire in your field, networking can help you build a strong professional network and establish yourself as a thought leader in your industry.

Finally, it's important to remember that innovation isn't just about coming up with new ideas – it's also about putting those ideas into action. This requires a willingness to take risks, a commitment to hard work, and the ability to learn from failure. By embracing innovation and taking bold steps to stand out in your field, you can position yourself for long-term success and achieve your career goals

Chapter Fourteen

Building a Meaningful Career

Finding purpose and meaning in your work

Work can be more than just a means of making a living; it can also be a source of purpose and fulfillment. However, finding that sense of purpose can be challenging, especially in today's fast-paced and ever-changing work environment.

One of the first steps to finding purpose in your work is to ask yourself what motivates you. What drives you to get out of bed every morning and go to work? For some, it may be the opportunity to make a difference in the world, while for others, it may be the chance to work with like-minded individuals. Once you have identified what motivates you, you can begin to explore ways to align your work with those motivations.

Another way to find purpose in your work is to focus on the impact that your work has on others. Whether you are a teacher helping students learn, a doctor saving lives, or a customer service representative providing assistance to customers, your work has an impact on the lives of others. By focusing on that impact and the positive outcomes you create, you can find a deeper sense of purpose and meaning in your work.

It is also important to consider how your work aligns with your personal values. If you value honesty, integrity, and respect, for example, you may not be fulfilled working for a company that doesn't share those values. By seeking out work that aligns with your values, you can find greater satisfaction and meaning in what you do.

Sometimes, finding purpose in your work may mean changing jobs or even careers. This can be a daunting prospect, but it can also be an opportunity to explore new interests and passions. Take the time to reflect on what you enjoy doing and what you are good at, and then explore career options that align with those strengths and interests. You may be surprised at the opportunities that are available to you.

Finally, it is important to remember that purpose and meaning are not always found in work alone. Finding purpose can also mean pursuing hobbies and interests outside of work, volunteering for causes you believe in, or spending time with family and friends. By finding balance between work and the rest of your life, you can create a sense of purpose and fulfillment that goes beyond your job title.

In today's fast-paced and often stressful work environment, finding purpose and meaning in your work can be a challenge. However, by focusing on your motivations, the impact you have on others, your personal values, and the balance between work and the rest of your life, you can find a deeper sense of purpose and fulfillment in what you do. Whether it means making small changes to your current job or exploring new career opportunities, the journey to finding purpose in your work is worth the effort.

Making a positive impact on your community and the world

As human beings, we all have an innate desire to make a difference in the world, to leave a lasting impact on those around us. This desire is what drives us to contribute to our communities and to engage in acts of kindness and compassion. When we make a positive impact on our community and the world, we not only improve the lives of others but also enhance our own sense of purpose and meaning.

There are countless ways to make a positive impact on your community and the world. Some people volunteer their time and skills to local charities and non-profit organizations, while others donate money to causes they care about. Some individuals take on leadership roles in their communities, working to effect change on a larger scale, while others simply strive to be a positive influence on those around them through small acts of kindness and generosity.

One of the most effective ways to make a positive impact on the world is by getting involved in causes that align with your personal values and beliefs. Perhaps you are passionate about environmental conservation, social justice, or education. Whatever your interests may be, there are countless organizations and initiatives that are working to create positive change in these areas. By getting involved with these groups and supporting their efforts, you can make a meaningful contribution to your community and the world.

Another way to make a positive impact is by simply being a positive force in your own community. This can mean volunteering at local events or participating in neighborhood clean-up efforts. It can also mean supporting local businesses and organizations, or simply being a friendly and supportive neighbor to those around you. By building strong relationships with those in your community, you can create a sense of connectedness and belonging that can have a ripple effect, improving the lives of everyone around you.

It's also important to recognize that making a positive impact on the world doesn't always require grand gestures or major commitments. Sometimes, the most impactful acts are the small ones – a smile, a kind word, or a thoughtful gesture. By taking the time to connect with others and show empathy and kindness, you can make a profound difference in someone's life.

Of course, making a positive impact on the world also requires a commitment to personal growth and development. This means continually learning and expanding your knowledge, skills, and perspectives so that you can be more effective in your efforts to create positive change. It also means being open to feedback and criticism, and using these experiences as opportunities for growth and self-improvement.

Finally, it's important to recognize that making a positive impact on the world is not something that can be accomplished overnight. It requires dedication, perseverance, and a willingness to stay committed to your goals even in the face of adversity. It may also require taking risks and stepping outside of your comfort zone, but the rewards can be immeasurable.

Making a positive impact on your community and the world is an important and worthwhile endeavor that can bring a sense of purpose and meaning to your life. Whether through volunteering, supporting local initiatives, or simply being a positive influence on those around you, there are countless ways to contribute to the greater good. By staying committed to your goals, continually learning and growing, and approaching challenges with a positive and proactive mindset, you can make a meaningful and lasting difference in the world.

Incorporating values and ethics into your career decisions

As we navigate our careers, it's important to consider not only our personal goals and aspirations, but also the impact our actions and decisions have on the world around us. Incorporating values and ethics into our career decisions is an essential step towards building a more just and equitable society.

When we talk about values and ethics in the workplace, we're referring to the set of beliefs and principles that guide our behavior and decision-making. These values might include honesty, integrity, respect for others, social responsibility, and a commitment to fairness and equality. By prioritizing these values in our professional lives, we can build careers that align with our personal beliefs and contribute to a better world.

One way to incorporate values and ethics into your career is to seek out opportunities that align with your values. For example, if you're passionate about environmental sustainability, you might look for jobs in the renewable energy sector or in organizations that prioritize sustainability in their operations. By working in a field that aligns with your values, you'll feel more fulfilled and motivated in your work, and you'll be making a positive impact on the world around you.

Another important way to incorporate values and ethics into your career is to hold yourself accountable for ethical behavior. This means taking responsibility for your actions and decisions, even when it's difficult or unpopular. It also means being transparent and honest in your communications, and treating others with respect and fairness. When you hold yourself to a high ethical standard, you not only build trust with your colleagues and clients, but you also set an example for others to follow.

It's also important to recognize that ethical dilemmas will arise in any career, and it's important to be prepared to handle them in a principled and thoughtful manner. This might involve seeking out guidance from a mentor or colleague, or seeking out resources and training on ethical decision-making. By proactively preparing for these challenges, you'll be better equipped to make difficult decisions and act in accordance with your values.

Another way to incorporate values and ethics into your career is to advocate for change within your organization or industry. This might involve speaking up when you see unethical behavior, or advocating for policies and practices that align with your values. By being an advocate for positive change, you can help create a more ethical and just workplace for yourself and your colleagues.

Finally, it's important to remember that incorporating values and ethics into your career is a lifelong process. As you gain experience and expertise, you'll likely encounter new challenges and opportunities to put your values into practice. By remaining committed to your principles and seeking out opportunities to make a positive impact, you can build a career that is both fulfilling and meaningful.

Incorporating values and ethics into your career decisions is not always easy, and it requires a willingness to challenge the status quo and take risks. But by prioritizing these principles, we can create more just and equitable workplaces and make a positive impact on the world around us. So whether you're just starting out in your career or looking to make a change, remember to stay true to your values and use them as a guide to build a career that is both successful and fulfilling.

Conclusion

As we come to the end of this journey, it's important to reflect on the key takeaways and lessons learned. Throughout this discussion, we've covered a variety of topics related to career development, personal growth, and making a positive impact in the world. Here are some of the main takeaways from our exploration:

1. Prioritize self-care and wellness: Taking care of yourself is critical to your success and well-being. Make time for rest, relaxation, and activities that bring you joy and fulfillment.

2. De-stress and recharge outside of work: Find ways to disconnect from work and engage in activities that help you relax and recharge. This can help improve your productivity and overall well-being.

3. Balance career goals with personal responsibilities and interests: It's important to find a balance between work and personal life. Take time to pursue your hobbies and interests and prioritize family and personal relationships.

4. Deal with setbacks and failures: Failure is a natural part of the process. Learn from your mistakes and use them as an opportunity to grow and improve.

5. Build resilience and bounce back from difficult situations: Resilience is a key trait that will help you navigate the ups and downs of your career. Develop coping mechanisms and a support system to help you get through tough times.

6. Find support and resources to help you overcome obstacles: You don't have to go through challenges alone. Seek out support from colleagues, mentors, and friends, and utilize resources like training programs and counseling services.

7. Stay up-to-date with industry trends and advancements: Staying current with industry developments is critical to remaining competitive in your field. Make an effort to stay informed and continuously learn and grow.

8. Embrace change and adapt to new technologies and work environments: The world is constantly changing, and it's important to be adaptable and flexible. Embrace new technologies and ways of working to stay ahead of the curve.

9. Find ways to innovate and stand out in your field: Creativity and innovation are essential for success in any field. Look for ways to bring fresh perspectives and ideas to your work.

10. Find purpose and meaning in your work: Ultimately, finding a sense of purpose and meaning in your work is what will keep you motivated and fulfilled. Take the time

to reflect on your values and passions and find ways to incorporate them into your career.

11. Make a positive impact on your community and the world: Use your skills and talents to make a difference in the world around you. Whether it's volunteering, mentoring, or engaging in activism, finding ways to give back can bring a sense of purpose and fulfillment.

12. Incorporate values and ethics into your career decisions: Make decisions that align with your values and principles, and prioritize ethics and integrity in all aspects of your work.

Incorporating these lessons into your career and personal life can help you lead a more fulfilling and successful life. Remember to prioritize self-care, seek support when needed, embrace change and innovation, and make a positive impact in the world. With these principles in mind, you can achieve your goals and make a meaningful difference in your career and beyond.

Congratulations! You have read this book almost to the end, and I hope you have received valuable information on how to build the career of your dreams.

Now, it's time to take action and start implementing these strategies. Don't let fear or uncertainty hold you back. Remember that building a successful career takes time, effort, and dedication, but the rewards are immeasurable.

Start by setting clear goals and priorities, and creating a plan of action to achieve them. Break down your goals into smaller, actionable steps, and celebrate your successes along the way.

Invest in your personal and professional development by staying up-to-date with industry trends, seeking out new learning opportunities, and finding mentors and role models who inspire you.

Take care of your mental and physical well-being by practicing self-care and finding ways to de-stress and recharge outside of work.

Embrace change and new technologies, and always be open to learning and adapting. This will not only keep you competitive in your field but also make you more resilient in the face of challenges.

Finally, remember to incorporate your values and ethics into your career decisions. Making a positive impact on your community and the world is not only fulfilling but also the right thing to do.

So, what are you waiting for? Start taking action today and build the career of your dreams. Whether you're just starting out or looking to make a change, with the right mindset, strategies, and support, you can achieve anything you set your mind to.

Remember, your dream career is within reach. All it takes is the courage to take the first step.

Dear readers,

As we come to the end of this journey together, I want to share some final thoughts and inspiration for the road ahead.

Building your dream career is not an easy feat, but it is possible. It takes hard work, dedication, and perseverance. Remember that success is not a destination, but a journey. Embrace the challenges and setbacks that come your way, and use them as opportunities for growth and learning.

Throughout this process, it's important to stay true to your values and ethics. These should be your guiding principles, helping you to make the right decisions and ensuring that you feel good about the work that you're doing. Never compromise on what you believe in, and always strive to make a positive impact on your community and the world.

As you embark on this journey, it's also crucial to stay up-to-date with industry trends and advancements. Innovation is key, and those who are willing to adapt and embrace change will thrive in their careers. Don't be afraid to take risks, and always be on the lookout for ways to differentiate yourself from others in your field.

Above all else, it's essential to find purpose and meaning in your work. Your career should not be a means to an end, but rather an extension of who you are and what you stand for. Take the time to reflect on your passions and interests, and seek out opportunities that align with your values.

Finally, I encourage you to take action and start building your dream career today. It's easy to get caught up in the planning and preparation, but at some point, you must take that first step. Don't let fear or doubt hold you back. You have the power to create a career that you love, one that brings you joy and fulfillment.

Remember that this journey is not a solitary one. Seek out mentors, peers, and resources to support you along the way. And when you encounter setbacks or challenges, don't be afraid to ask for help.

I wish you all the best as you embark on this exciting journey. May you find joy, purpose, and success in all that you do.

Sincerely,

Harper James